DEBATING GUN CONTROL

DEBATING ETHICS

General Editor
Christopher Heath Wellman
Washington University of St. Louis

Debating Ethics is a series of volumes in which leading scholars defend opposing views on timely ethical questions and core theoretical issues in contemporary moral, political, and legal philosophy.

Debating the Ethics of Immigration
Is There a Right to Exclude?
Christopher Heath Wellman and Philip Cole

Debating Brain Drain
May Governments Restrict Emigration?
Gillian Brock and Michael Blake

Debating Procreation
Is It Wrong to Reproduce?
David Benatar and David Wasserman

Debating Climate Ethics
Stephen Gardiner and David Weisbach

Debating Gun Control
How Much Regulation Do We Need?
David DeGrazia and Lester H. Hunt

Debating Gun Control

How Much Regulation Do We Need?

DAVID DEGRAZIA

AND

LESTER H. HUNT

OXFORD
UNIVERSITY PRESS

OXFORD
UNIVERSITY PRESS

Oxford University Press is a department of the University of Oxford. It furthers the University's objective of excellence in research, scholarship, and education by publishing worldwide. Oxford is a registered trade mark of Oxford University Press in the UK and certain other countries.

Published in the United States of America by Oxford University Press 198 Madison Avenue, New York, NY 10016, United States of America.

Library of Congress Cataloging-in-Publication Data
Names: DeGrazia, David, author. | Hunt, Lester H., 1946- author.
Title: Debating gun control : how much regulation do we need? / David DeGrazia and Lester H. Hunt.
Description: New York : Oxford University Press, [2016] | Series: Debating ethics | Description based on print version record and CIP data provided by publisher; resource not viewed.
Identifiers: LCCN 2016017777 (print) | LCCN 2016010462 (ebook) | ISBN 9780190251277 (Updf) | ISBN 9780190251284 (Epub) | ISBN 9780190629465 (Online) | ISBN 9780190251260 (pbk. : alk. paper) | ISBN 9780190251253 (hardcover : alk. paper)
Subjects: LCSH: Gun control—United States. | Firearms ownership—United States. | Firearms—Law and legislation—United States.
Classification: LCC HV7436 (print) | LCC HV7436 .D446 2016 (ebook) | DDC 363.330973—dc23
LC record available at https://lccn.loc.gov/2016017777

1 3 5 7 9 8 6 4 2

Paperback printed by Webcom Inc., Canada
Hardback printed by Bridgeport National Bindery, Inc., United States of America

For everyone who is interested in an intelligent and civil discussion

CONTENTS

PART II THE CASE IN FAVOR
by David DeGrazia

ACKNOWLEDGMENTS

Many people have worked to make this book possible. Among them, both authors would especially like to thank Peter Ohlin and Lucy Randall of Oxford University Press and Kit Wellman, editor of the Debating Ethics book series. In addition, David DeGrazia would like to thank his wife, Kathleen Smith, and daughter, Zoe, for their love and encouragement. Lester Hunt would like to thank Deborah and Nat for all their support and in addition he would like to thank the librarians at the Oregon Public Library in Oregon, Wisconsin, for ignoring him as he sat in an alcove day after day writing his contribution to this book.

INTRODUCTION

David DeGrazia

and

Lester H. Hunt

A gun, or firearm, is a portable weapon with a metal tube from which projectiles can be propelled at high speed by an explosive force. Guns are designed, among other things, to be able to deliver lethal force with greater precision than is possible with some weapons such as bombs, missiles, and cannons. In the United States, firearms are commonly owned for such legal and widely accepted purposes as self-defense in the home, target shooting, and hunting. At the same time, guns are frequently the weapon of choice in suicides and are often used for such criminal purposes as burglary, robbery, and murder.

Guns occupy an ambivalent place in American culture. On the one hand, the United States leads all nations in rates of private gun ownership, indicating considerable enthusiasm for these weapons. On the other hand, stories of gun tragedies frequently make the news, provoking questions about whether high gun ownership rates and liberal gun policies are partly responsible for the fact that the United States has, among developed nations, relatively high homicide and suicide rates. The American gun lobby exerts enormous political power, so even those legislators who firmly believe in stricter gun regulations rarely take steps in that direction. But the public, as distinct from its elected officials, continues to debate.

The debate tends to be acrimonious and is frequently misinformed and illogical. The main question that is disputed concerns the topic of this book: gun control. Strictly speaking, the question is not whether there should be *any* regulations setting limits on the ownership and use of firearms. After all, to provide just one example, it would be bizarre to deny that young children should be prohibited from owning and using machine guns. The real question is *the extent* to which federal or state governments should regulate gun ownership and use in the interest of public safety. Yet, in common discourse, those who favor relatively minimal gun regulations—such as those prevailing in federal law today—are described as *opposing* gun control, while only those who favor significantly more extensive gun regulations are described as being *in favor of* gun control. The title of this book reflects this common usage. The two authors are said to be "debating gun control," whereas it might be less misleading, at least to some people, to say that we are debating relatively minimal gun regulations and relatively extensive ones, respectively.

In debating this important topic, we are committed to elevating the quality of discussion from the levels that usually prevail in the public arena. Both authors have been trained and—for many years—employed in the discipline of academic philosophy, a discipline that prizes intellectual honesty, respect for opposing views, command of relevant facts, and rigorous reasoning. We hope to bring the advantages of philosophical analysis to this highly charged issue in the service of illuminating the strongest possible cases for and against (relatively extensive) gun regulations and finding whatever common ground may exist between these positions.

It also bears emphasis that this is a book about the *ethics* of gun control. Neither author, in developing his position, ignores current American laws about guns; nor does either imagine that an ethical debate should proceed without awareness of the political climate that provides much of its context. Rather, the point is that our debate about gun control is about *the shape of morally defensible, or morally responsible, gun policy*. It is worthwhile to address the ethics of gun policy because (1) the wisdom and legitimacy of existing laws can always be challenged from an ethical standpoint, and (2) the existing legal framework—for example, the (currently asserted) constitutional right to private gun ownership—leaves many specific matters undetermined, such as which specific limits to this right would represent responsible policy options. Moreover, legal rights are often thought to enjoy the support of moral (or human) rights. Had the U.S. Supreme Court recently decided that the American Constitution did *not* support a right to private gun ownership, many gun advocates would have believed that the decision violated their moral (or human) right to gun ownership. Thus, legal analysis does not capture all that is important about the shape of appropriate public policy. Our book addresses the ethical dimension.

The organization of this book is very simple. Following this introduction, Lester Hunt presents his case against (more-than-minimal) gun control. After this presentation, David DeGrazia makes his case for (moderately extensive) gun control. Readers are left to decide for themselves which position is more defensible and cogent. We hope as well that readers will be motivated to take the civil tone of this book and the emphasis on factual evidence and logical reasoning into any public discussions about guns that they may enter.

In making his case against gun control, Lester Hunt begins by analyzing the term "gun control" and finds that when properly defined, it does single out a real issue and one that really is at the center of the debate that is waged around it. This is the question of whether guns belong to that class of things (which may include alcohol, other psychoactive drugs, nude dancing, and prostitution) that might be too prevalent, too widely available, so that the quantity that ought to exist might be either zero or some amount that is significantly less than the present one. It is the idea that there can be "too many" guns, and that an important role of gun regulation is to restrict their availability. Understood in this way, Hunt argues, the debate about gun control can serve as an illuminating focal point for some profound issues of very general interest, including the role of free will as opposed to the influence of the human-made portion of our environment, and the role of notions of risk and risk reduction in the formulation of sound public policy. The core of Hunt's argument against gun control is rights-based: the right to own a gun is a necessary consequence of a more basic right, which is that of self-defense. In this way, it is like the right to

own a telephone or an Internet device, which are consequences of the right of free expression. He concludes with
a discussion of the politics of the gun control debate. The
position he offers here is compatible with reasonable gun
regulations that are not currently on the books, including universal background checks and possibly even licensing of owners—these, after all, are not aimed at reducing
the sheer quantity of guns in private hands but, rather, at
changing the users among whom firearms are distributed.
However, the public debate on such moderate measures is
corrupted by a failure of trust on the part of anti-control
advocates in the motives that would lie behind further
regulations: a failure of trust that is unfortunately more or
less justified by the facts.

Following Hunt's case against gun control, David
DeGrazia develops his case in favor. After briefly char-
acterizing the American status quo with respect to gun
violence and gun policy, he clarifies his point of ethical
focus: the shape of morally defensible policy on gun *ownership*; space limitations preclude addressing the carrying of guns in public or the ethics of hunting. Next, he
examines the Second Amendment to the Constitution,
presents reasons to question the Supreme Court's recent
reading of this amendment as conferring a right to private firearm ownership, and notes that even the court
acknowledged the compatibility of gun rights and gun
control. Following this legal analysis, DeGrazia's ethical
case for gun control begins negatively—with critiques of
(1) appeals to physical security and (2) appeals to various liberties as bases for arguments against gun control.
The case for gun control proceeds, more positively, to a
consequentialist argument and a rights-based argument.

The consequentialist argument stresses the importance of public safety and underscores the tendency of gun ownership for personal safety to be self-defeating. The rights-based argument emphasizes the need for proper *enforcement* of a right not to be shot and children's right not to harmed as a result of gross negligence, and invokes a right to a reasonably safe environment, which justifies limits on the (assumed) right to gun ownership. The completed case for gun control is followed by a discussion of American gun politics. This political discussion helps to explain the current, rather extreme state of American gun policy and highlights the distinction between what is politically feasible and what is morally defensible. DeGrazia's contribution concludes with suggestions for morally defensible gun policy.

DEBATING GUN CONTROL

PART I

THE CASE AGAINST

LESTER H. HUNT

What Is the Issue of Gun Control About?

■ □ ■

WHAT IS "GUN CONTROL"? WHY would anyone be against such a thing? Surely there should be constraining laws that apply to firearms. How, then, can the question of whether we ought to have "gun control" be controversial? The simplest answer to that question, I think, is that not all such laws are included when people argue about something they call gun control. Are safety regulations, such as ones aimed to ban guns that might accidentally discharge, instances of gun control? How about laws that prohibit guns to a class of people—such as children below a certain age, convicted criminals, or people with a history of some relevant sort of mental illness—on grounds that they are deemed to be insufficiently trustworthy users of these weapons? If excluding certain classes of owners is not gun control, what about laws that exclude a class of guns such as handguns, or certain features or accessories of weapons such as silencers, or capabilities to deliver multiple rounds with a single pull of the trigger or more than a certain number of rounds without reloading? Surely not all these things are among those about which we disagree when we disagree about gun control. But if not all attempts to control the ownership and use of firearms by law qualify as "gun control," then what does the term mean, if anything? Should the term itself be retired as a useless, perhaps even as a worse-than-useless source of confusion and sower of discord?

No doubt, there are some terms that do deserve to be sent into retirement for reasons like this. The word *fascism*, for instance, might be an attractive candidate for this sort of treatment. It is a word that once was useful and had a fairly precise meaning, but after years of being used as a propagandistic stick to beat up on people whose politics we do not like, it has retained its emotional power while ceasing to have any definite meaning outside the relatively small community of serious scholars. Some words harm public discourse more than they help it.

However, though the expression "gun control" is hardly pellucidly clear, I do not think it belongs in this category of expressions. It is not abusive or emotionally loaded. It does not favor one side of the debate at the expense of the other. Indeed, one often sees it used by both sides of the controversy. We hear people saying they are against gun control, and we hear people saying with equal passion, and using the same phrase, that they are for it. More important, I think the phrase does capture something of the core of the debate, and with just a little stipulation it might be defined in a way that makes it reasonably lucid and useful.

Surely, everyone who has observed the controversy about gun control has noticed that among the combatants there is often a sharp and profound conflict between their attitudes toward guns themselves. To some extent this a difference of feeling, even of passion, but I believe it also reflects an underlying issue that is a matter of logic and theory, as well as emotion. It seems to me that, at the core of the debate, sometimes hidden below the surface, lurks a very real disagreement about what we might call the moral status of guns themselves. For purposes of this discussion, I will say that the moral status of a thing lies in the fact that there are features of the thing indicating that, by its very nature, it is morally suspect and questionable—or indeed, the opposite of this, that it is somehow privileged by moral considerations that concern the very nature of the thing. In the case of guns, the possibility that will be most obvious to many educated people will be that the status of guns is of the former, negative sort. "Guns," as Hugh LaFollette reminds us in presenting his own defense of gun control, "were invented for the military, they were designed to cause (and threaten) harm."[1] He takes their unique nature to imply that they are things legitimately liable to get a special sort of treatment at the hands of the coercive power of the state. I would point out that there are other things often treated this way, including, for example, pornography, alcohol, tobacco, and various other psychoactive drugs. In addition to objects or substances, some services are often treated similarly, such as prostitution, nude dancing, gambling, and abortion.[2] When such goods and services are not prohibited altogether, like cocaine, they are subject to laws that make them less available, as is usually the case with alcoholic beverages. Often, their sale is legally restricted to those who are specifically licensed by the state to sell them. Again, alcoholic beverages are clearly a case in point. The function of such licensure laws is not to limit provision of the good or service to providers who are qualified by some special expertise. Rather, these laws are intended to limit provision—period. Similarly, public authorities might, perhaps by means of zoning regulations, limit the geographic areas in which sales may be made. They might also prohibit sales during certain hours of the day or certain days of the week, or they might place burdensome "sin taxes" on their sale. Some laws that fall short of outright prohibitions on a good or service nonetheless place various hurdles and speed bumps in the path of consumers who want access to them. They function to make such goods and services less available than they otherwise would be. Obviously, the thinking behind such laws is that some goods or services are the sort of thing that should not be too readily available, that there is an ever-present possibility society has "too much" of that good or service. We can think of outright bans on these goods or services as simply constituting the extreme case of laws of this sort. Those who advocate such bans believe that *any* amount of those goods or services is too much.

Obviously, many people see guns as belonging in this category: they are apt to say things like "there are too many guns out there,"[3] and that a solution to such problems would be laws that restrict "the availability of guns." I propose defining gun control legislation as being this sort of law; that is, it is legislation that either is intended to treat guns, or some major class of guns, this way or is best justified by arguments that support such treatment. Laws that forbid guns to a class of unreliable users, such as children or violent criminals, do not qualify as cases of gun control because they are based on considerations about the users and not primarily about the thing used. It is equally clear, though for a different sort of reason, that safety regulations do not qualify as cases of gun control, since they do not make guns less widely available but, rather, (if they are successful) more safe.

It is less clear whether, on my definition, banning magazines or clips that hold more than a certain number of rounds of ammunition qualifies as gun control. This does not necessarily mean that there is something wrong with my definition. There is such a thing as a definition's being too clear, especially when it is meant to capture a concept in ordinary language and to clarify the scope of public disputes for which that concept is fundamental. After all, one of the things that people are apt to disagree about when such bans are debated is whether or not such bans are indeed cases of gun control. This is obviously true of magazine/clip size. Given that this question may be a meaningful one, and not just a quibble about words, it may be best not to foreclose it at the outset with an arbitrary stipulative definition. If it is possible to settle the issue with substantive arguments, then it is best to wait and see what those arguments might be.

In the remainder of these chapters, when I speak of "gun control," I refer to *restrictionist* regulation of guns— regulation that is either deliberately aimed at or best justified by the purpose of restricting their availability to ordinary adult citizens. The attitude toward guns that undergirds gun control, thus defined, is a familiar one, and it is surely not difficult to sympathize with it. If we follow the line of thought suggested by the remark by LaFollette, and think of guns in terms of the intention with which they were originally invented or the intentions behind the way they are continually redesigned and improved, one can easily see how one would think their very inception is morally special, so to speak, and not special in a good way.

They are conceived and intended to destroy—if not people or animals, then some other sort of target. They are conceived in destruction, and if this does not quite mean that they are conceived in sin, then at least it might support the idea that they are liable to special treatment by the coercive powers of the state.

This sort of idea gains even more support if we think of guns, not in terms of the intentions with which they are created and improved by inventors and engineers, but in terms of the role they play within the intentions, values, and overriding goals of the civilians who possess them. The factor I have in mind is most pronounced and conspicuous in the case of handguns, which are not popular for use in hunting. If a civilian possesses a handgun, it is in some cases for use in crime or, in many more cases, in self-protection against crime. Even the latter of these two purposes is one that some will find disturbing. If I acquire the means of lethal force for the purpose of possible use against a human being then, even for a legitimate defensive use, I am thinking of my relations with my fellow human beings in a certain way. A gun is a tool, a product of human technology; and like any technological device, it exists to solve problems. If the problem that needs to be solved exists between the gun owner and another human being, it is obvious that the imagined solution rests on some disturbing assumptions. The owner assumes that there are situations with absolute, irresolvable conflicts of interests—or at least, of desires—between human beings. In such situations, there is no appeal to reason, no compromise acceptable to all parties, no consensus to be reached. The only option is to resort to force. Worse, the owner is assuming that it may be beyond the power of the state to preempt this use of force—to make it unnecessary for one to protect oneself. These are very disturbing thoughts, though it is impossible to deny they are true.

There is one very obvious alternative to the view of the inherent moral status of guns as I have described it. This would be to maintain that it is, quite literally, nonsensical to attribute a moral status to mere inanimate objects, that this is as true of guns as it is of any other mere thing. One can morally evaluate human actions, human individuals, and groups and organizations of individuals (Planned Parenthood, the National Rifle Association, etc.), but not things. People have moral attributes, but guns are morally neutral. This view of the matter no doubt animates some of the anti-restrictionist movement. Conservative columnist Victor Davis Hanson wrote during the debate that followed the Sandy Hook, Connecticut, school shooting: "Like a knife or bomb, a gun is a tool, and the human who misuses it is the only guilty party."[4] The same thought is conveyed by the familiar saying, "Guns don't kill people, people kill people."

However, plausible though it is, there is another, quite different attitude that seems to be expressed in much of the anti-control literature. It would be difficult to prove beyond a doubt that this attitude is as widespread as I believe it is, and would probably be resisted by many in the pro-control camp as wildly counterintuitive, but it seems to me that many in the other camp view guns not as neutral but as positively good. Strange as this view will seem to some readers of this book, I think those who fail to understand that view will fail to understand important features of the gun control debate. This is true of both sides of the debate: failure to grasp the attitudes that underlie a position cause us to see some participants as unreasonable at best and as fools, lunatics, or scoundrels at worst, rather than as the basically rational and well-meaning people they generally are.[5] The basis of the view that guns are good is the same in kind as the basis of the anti-gun view: for the partisans of this view, guns are by their nature entangled in a dense network of intentions, values, and overriding goals. The view is rooted in part in the fact that a gun, like any other technological device, is a freedom-extender: it enables one to do things that one could not otherwise do. This simple fact supports a link between this particular technology and an important moral value: responsibility for the rights of the innocent, both one's own rights and those of others. Large corporations routinely hire armed guards to protect their property and the lives and bodies of their customers from the depredations of criminals. Small businesses typically cannot afford to do this. In place of such professional services they are apt to substitute self-protection, often in the form of a gun kept on the premises.

In the pro-gun literature, these simple facts connect gun ownership with a powerful array of moral ideas and ideals. The divide between the pro- and the anti- sides of this debate is so great that many on the anti- side will wonder what "ideals" could possibly be involved in owning a gun for purposes of shooting people—even allowing that the "shooting" is unlikely in any one case to actually happen and that the "people" involved are attackers and invaders of someone's home or business.

Eloquent fragments of an answer to this question can be found in an essay by Washington attorney Jeffrey

Snyder, an essay that is frequently cited and much admired in the anti-restrictionist community:

> For years, feminists have labored to educate people that rape is not about sex, but about domination, degradation, and control. Evidently, someone needs to inform the law enforcement establishment and the media that kidnapping, robbery, carjacking, and assault are not about property.
>
> Crime is not only a complete disavowal of the social contract, but also a commandeering of the victim's person and liberty. If the individual's dignity lies in the fact that he is a moral agent engaging in actions of his own will, in free exchange with others, then crime always violates the victim's dignity. It is, in fact, an act of enslavement. Your wallet, your purse, or your car may not be worth your life, but your dignity is; and if it is not worth fighting for, it can hardly be said to exist.[6]

It should come as no surprise that the anti-gun, pro-control literature is strongly focused on the evils of violence—in particular on the suffering, injury, and death caused by guns. It might be more surprising that the pro-gun, anti-control side is also focused on, even obsessed with, the evils of violence and of acute or chronic threats of violence. Yet the way in which the two literatures view the evil of violence is quite different. Granted that violence is evil, what is evil *about* it? Note that Snyder's comments speak not of injury and suffering but, rather, in terms that are more suggestive of degradation and defilement. On this view, the evil of crime is its violation of one's dignity, presumably because it compels what is yours—your car, your wallet, perhaps your body—to serve the purposes of the criminal, in complete disregard of your purposes, just as if you were a mere passive thing with no goals of your own. Crime violates your dignity by violating your autonomy. A remedy for such violations is *agency*: seizing control of your own life and employing what is rightfully yours to serve your own, legitimate purposes. Thus, though it may be much better to live a life where defending your rights is not something you have to do for yourself (perhaps because you are wealthy enough to live in a low-crime area or to pay others to do it for you), there are good reasons why arming yourself for protection is not an entirely regrettable option. Such reasons are rooted in principles that are fundamentally ethical.

Students of philosophy will have noticed a certain kinship between the notions I have attributed to Snyder's line of reasoning and those central to the ethics of Immanuel Kant. I don't think the question of whether these notions are really and truly in the spirit of the Kantian tradition need concern us here. The resemblance is enough to suggest that some of the notions involved are not only ethical but, indeed, rooted in the moral thinking of modern Western liberalism. Among the divides underlying the gun control debate is one between two sides of the liberal tradition. One side focuses on the liberal value of empathy for injury and suffering, while the other emphasizes the equally liberal ideas of dignity and autonomy. I am tempted to call the former tradition "compassion-based," but for the fact that both are based on compassion of a sort.[7] What each has compassion *for* is somewhat different, though. For the former, what is important is rescuing human beings from pain, while the latter places importance on repairing individual dignity and self-respect. I, personally, have a good deal of sympathy for the dignity and self-respect side of this divide, but for the moment that is not my point. Rather, I urge the reader to understand that the gun debate is separated by contrasting ethical ideas, and that unless we keep this in mind we are apt to seriously miss the point of the debate.[8]

I believe that these moral ideas just mentioned, especially those of dignity and autonomy, are relevant to a subject that always seems to come up when Americans discuss the right to arms: the Second Amendment to the U.S. Constitution. As everyone knows, this amendment is rather curiously worded and punctuated: "A well regulated Militia, being necessary to the security of a free State, the right of the people to keep and bear Arms, shall not be infringed." Much has been written on what this bit of eighteenth-century prose is supposed to mean. In particular, its seemingly gratuitous mention of the now-obsolete military (or para-military) institution of the citizen militia has sucked up whole seas of ink. A plausible and widespread view is that the mention of the militia is essential to its meaning: that in so far as it grants a right to arms, this right is a means and the citizen militia is the end. Now that militias are obsolete and we have a thoroughly professional military, the right, in this view of the matter, is also obsolete. It was not an individual right at all but, rather, a group right: a right to bear arms as a member of a militia. Insofar as it was a right, this right was really just a means to a now-obsolete military end.

I think a case can be made that, although the mention of militias is essential to understanding the meaning of this odd sentence, this widespread view draws the wrong conclusion. As a matter of history, it has the issue almost exactly backwards.

There is no way to understand this issue without knowing something of this peculiar institution—the militias. As Daniel J. Boorstin tells of it in his magisterial study, *The Americans*, the citizen militia must have impressed Europeans as "a prime example of American 'regression,'" as it was a revival of the medieval Assize of Arms, which dates from 1181 in England.[9] The basic idea was that all able-bodied free men (in the colonies, this generally included servants who were not slaves) were to be available for defense of the community on short notice. This obligation included a duty to arm oneself, an obligation that sometimes was quite detailed on such matters as how much powder and bullets one had to carry. Militia members were not uniformed, and even their unit leaders were often not military personnel. One of the most unmilitary features of militia units—each of which was centered on a particular town or village—was their common practice of selecting officers by a vote of the members. The presence of the militia accounted for one of the most distinctive features of the colonies: the complete absence of any regular, professional military.

Perhaps the oddest thing about the militia system was that it never really made much sense in purely military terms. Its extreme decentralization, informality, and general lack of discipline and professional deportment caused a host of military problems. The close identification that a given militia unit had with the interest and fate of the town that was its base was a major obstruction to large-scale planning. Militia men would often simply pull up stakes and leave, regardless of military context, as soon as their promised tour of duty was completed. Outright desertion was commonplace. Washington frequently lamented the "want of perseverance which characterizes all militia." This comment is typical of many:

> I solemnly declare I never was witness to a single instance that can countenance an opinion of Militia or raw troops being fit for the real business of fighting. I have found them useful as light Parties to skirmish in the woods, but incapable of making or sustaining a serious attack.... The late battle of Camden is a melancholy comment upon this doctrine. The militia fled at the first fire, and left the Continental Troops surrounded on every side, and over-powered by numbers to combat for safety instead of victory.

At the siege of Newport, five thousand militia men deserted. At another crucial moment in the war, General Edward Stevens begged the militia men under his command to stay "a few days" until reinforcements could arrive,

> [b]ut to my great mortification and astonishment [he said] scarce a man would agree to do it, and gave for answer he was a good soldier that served his time out. If the salvation of the country had depended on their staying ten or fifteen days, I don't believe they would have done it. Militia won't do. Their greatest study is to rub through their tour of duty with whole bones.

And yet, among nonmilitary leaders and intellectuals, the general level of approval for the militia as an institution remained high—long after it would seem that logic and the facts could any longer support such an attitude. Indeed, the Second Amendment itself, with the comment about its "being necessary to the security of a free State," is itself an expression of this attitude. At the same time, its phrase "a well-regulated militia" reflected a forlorn hope, also very common, that in military terms this institution might somehow be made to perform better than, as a matter of plain fact, it ever had. No doubt the phrase about a *free* state contains an important hint that the reasons this hope persisted as long as it did were not ultimately military but political and moral. My point here is a fairly simple one: that the fact that the amendment gives the alleged need for the militia as a reason for the right to bear arms, together with the fact that the institution has become militarily obsolete, does not imply that the founders' reason for this right is also obsolete, since the reason for their attachment to this institution could not have been primarily military.[10] It seems to me that reasons are subject to a certain transitivity rule: if the reason for x is y, and the reason for y is z, then the reason (or, you could call it the real reason or the ultimate reason) for x is z. The reason for the right to arms in the Second Amendment is not the militias but, rather, something further—something that is not obviously obsolete.

As to what the ultimate reasons in this case might have been, I need not inquire at length here, though a comment made by President Timothy Dwight of Yale early in the nineteenth century suggests it involves the notion that widespread ownership of firearms by the citizenry is a sign of political health and, to some extent, a good in and of itself:

> To trust arms in the hands of the people at large has, in Europe, been believed ... to be an experiment fraught only with danger. Here by a long trial it has been proved to be perfectly harmless.... If the government be equitable; if it be reasonable in its exactions; if proper attention be

paid to the education of children in knowledge, and religion, few men will be disposed to use arms, unless for their amusement, and for the defense of themselves and their country. The difficulty, here, has been to persuade the citizens to keep arms; not to prevent them from being employed for violent purposes.[11]

By the time of the Second Amendment, the nations of Europe had long been pursuing policies of weapons restrictionism, while the new nation of the Americas had been doing more or less the opposite. As we can see from Dwight's comments, the Americans were pursuing their own policy as part of a wider, positive political ideal: a distinctive notion of a sound polity as a free state. In any full explanation of this positive ideal, the notions of the dignity and autonomy of the individual, or some very closely related ideas, would inevitably play a crucial role. It is in such a context that this curiously worded amendment, as a matter of history, must be understood.

NOTES

1. Hugh LaFollette, "Gun Control" *Ethics* 110 (January 2000): 269.
2. Here I am parting company with LaFollette (see n. 1). His view is that guns are liable to special treatment simply because they are "inherently dangerous" objects, a class from which, surprisingly, he excludes alcohol, tobacco, and automobiles ("Gun Control," 269). Incidentally, the idea of inherently dangerous objects and activities is also to be found in the law. I will discuss the legal version of the idea in chapter 6. It will be obvious to readers of LaFollette's article that the legal version is very different from LaFollette's.

3. Actually, this quote is one I saw projected on my TV screen as I took a break from writing this page. It is a quote from an interview that actor Liam Neeson had given that day. His choice of words, as it turned out, was a big stronger and may be found at Nisha Chittal, "Liam Neeson: U.S. Has "too many F—ing Guns," MSNBC website, January 15, 2015, http://www.msnbc.com/msnbc/liam-neeson-america-has-too-many-f-ing-guns. His comments are worth quoting in full, as they express at least one important element of the view I am trying to capture here: "There's too many f—ing guns out there. Especially in America. I think the population is like, 320 million? There's over 300 million guns. Privately owned, in America. I think it's a f—ing disgrace. Every week now we're picking up a newspaper and seeing, 'Yet another few kids have been killed in schools.'" Given that these comments were made apropos of a terrorist murder of the staff of *Charlie Hebdo*, a satirical magazine in France, a country with strong gun control laws and relatively few guns privately owned, I think this should be taken as evidence of a deep underlying attitude and not a rational response to then-current circumstances.

4. "The War between the Amendments," National Review Online website, January 17, 2013, http://m.nationalreview.com/articles/337906/war-between-amendments-victor-davis-hanson.

5. Arnold Kling, *The Three Languages of Politics* (Amazon Digital Services, 2013). "Amazon Digital Services" is available at http://www.amazon.com/.

6. Jeffrey Snyder, "A Nation of Cowards," in Robert Muth, ed., *Guns in America: A Reader* (New York: New York University Press, 1999), 182–93. Originally published in *The Public Interest* 113 (Fall 1993).

7. In the case of the pro-restrictionist literature, I think I can take this to be obvious. As a recent example from the other side of the divide that deserves special mention is Chris Bird, *Thank God I Had a Gun: True Accounts of Self-Defense*, 2nd ed. (San Antonio: Privateer Publications, 2014). It consists of reports, based on original research by the author

(a professional journalist), of sixteen cases of citizens who were threatened, injured, or in some instances terrorized by criminals and who defended themselves with firearms. One thing that makes the stories gripping is the author's compassion for the citizens (even, in some cases, for their attackers), but the focus of this empathy is, it seems to me, as I describe it here.

8. For a mind-expanding discussion of the roots and manifold varieties of such misunderstandings, see Johnathan Haidt, *The Righteous Mind: How Good People Are Divided by Politics and Religion* (New York: Random House, 2012).

9. Daniel J. Boorstin, *The Americans. Volume 1: The Colonial Experience* (New York: Random House, 1958), 354. This paragraph and the one that follows are based on pp. 352–72 of Boorstin's book.

10. My point here is consistent with the more obvious logical point that, as Stephen Halbrook puts it, "the purpose clause does not negate the right." That is, from the fact that the reason given for the right (militias) no longer applies, it does not follow that the right no longer applies, unless this was the *only* reason—an idea that is not indicated in the text at all. To suppose that, as a matter of logic, it does follow, is to commit the fallacy of denying the antecedent. From the propositions $P \rightarrow Q$ and $-P$, $-Q$ does not follow. Stephen P. Halbrook, *The Founders' Second Amendment: Origins of the Right to Bear Arms* (Chicago: Ivan R. Dee, 2008), 332–34.

11. Boorstin, *The Americans*, 1: 352–53.

2

Arguments Based on Rights and Arguments Based on Facts

■ □ ■

IN THE UNITED STATES, DISCUSSIONS of gun control are often framed in terms of rights. To some extent this is no doubt due to the Second Amendment to the Constitution, which I briefly discussed in chapter 1. However we might want to resolve the legal issues that the amendment raises, one thing that discussions of gun regulations must live with is that, in our culture, such issues are dominated by the question of whether there is a human right that resolves the main policy issue: a "right to keep and bear arms."

At the same time, there is a tendency in our culture to approach issues in a way that contrasts sharply with framing them in terms of rights, an approach that you might naturally think of as basing one's discussion on purely factual considerations. This immediately raises an obvious question: "If people have a certain right, isn't it a fact that they do? What, then, is the difference between matters of right and matters of fact?" I think I can side-step this question simply by saying that, for purposes of this part of this book, "facts" refers to the sort of thing we discover by means of the sophisticated methods of modern natural and social sciences: controlled experiments, statistical surveys, clinical trials, regression analysis, and the like. We do not find out whether people have a certain right by such methods as these. How, then, do we "find out" whether people have a certain right? Serious academic discussions of such issues are typically carried out by means of a procedure called "reflective equilibrium." It involves trying to bring our unreflective judgments (often called "intuitions") about a given issue into some coherent relationship with our general, principled beliefs about it. We attempt to formulate general principles or definitions that account for these judgments and test these principles against other judgments with which they seem to clash (possible counter-examples to the principle or definition). We can respond to the clash either by revising the general notion or by abandoning the judgment. This can lead to further revisions and abandonments. The procedure is called an equilibrium process because it aims at a theoretically possible point at which we no longer have good reason to make changes, which would be a state of equilibrium. This method can become complex and sophisticated, but at no point does it resemble the process by which scientists discover "facts" (in my sense of the word).

The argument I will offer here is of the rights-based sort and will use the reflective equilibrium approach to the issue. As a professor of philosophy I have had a great deal of experience with arguments of this sort. Like most people who teach humanistic subjects, I have had no professional training in the sophisticated methods by which contemporary social scientists establish the facts that are relevant to public policy issues. My own opinion is that humanists who offer arguments primarily based on such methods typically do not do a very good job of it. I will not be offering an argument of that sort. Though I will need to say something about the sorts of considerations that I have placed under the loose-fitting label of "the facts," the focus of my argument will be on matters about which I think I am competent to make a case that deserves to be taken seriously: questions about individual rights.

I suppose I should also say something about the particular conception of individual rights I will be using; a brief comment now might prevent a large misunderstanding later on. One possible source of ideas here would be the sort of radical libertarianism that is inspired by the structure of rights John Locke sets forth in his *Second Treatise of Government*.[1] Locke held that one has rights that amount to a sort of absolute sovereignty over one's own self, one's mind and body—rights that he consistently speaks of as a sort of property right. This sovereignty extends to rights over the things of this world, provided only that one comes to possess them honestly: my right to my honestly acquired property may be infringed by the state only if the infringement is necessary (necessary, not merely helpful) to carry out the most basic function of the state, which is to maintain public order by defending these Lockean sovereignty-rights against violation.[2] This approach to individual rights would seem to make short work of the issue of gun ownership. It would seem to imply immediately that the state may not take away the honestly acquired firearms of law-abiding citizens—at least if we suppose that there has been no general, massive breakdown of law and order of the sort that would justify a declaration of martial law. Obviously,

4

Option-Rights and Means-Rights

■ □ ■

OBVIOUSLY, THE RIGHT OF SELF-DEFENSE is not the same thing as the right to own a gun. What is the relation between them? As I have suggested in the preceding chapters, my view on this issue is, to put it a little vaguely for the moment, that they are related in such a way that the former right implies the latter one. I will argue, eventually, that the issue of the relation between these two rights can be understood as an instance of a broader issue of the relation between two classes of rights, which I will call option-rights and means-rights. The broader issue is one of more general interest than that of a gun owner's rights and is one reason the issue of gun ownership is interesting and worth thinking about.

First, as to the narrower question, I think we can gain some insight by briefly looking at one of the court cases that eventually led to the *McDonald* decision, which was the later of the two Supreme Court cases I mentioned in chapter 3. This is *National Rifle Association v. Chicago* (2009), which was decided by the Seventh District Court of Appeals. The opinion handed down by this distinguished panel of judges

the people of the economically advanced nations of the world are far from living under such conditions today.

I have to confess that I, personally, have a great deal of sympathy for this view of rights, but I cannot use it here. Though it is obviously very constraining in the limits it places on legitimate government activity, most people do not seem to find it obviously true, at least if we can judge on the basis of the sorts of governments they tolerate and even support. If I were to rest my argument on this admittedly "extreme" doctrine, I would have to spend most of my effort trying to convince readers that the doctrine itself is true, which would mean writing an essay mainly on the theoretical foundations of individual rights and not mainly on the issue of guns.

Fortunately, there is an alternative approach that will serve my purposes here at least as well as this one while hauling less theoretical baggage. It is the conception of rights that dominates our culture in Western liberal democracies, and it can be found, among other places, in decisions handed down by the U.S. Supreme Court. This view allows the possibility that some rights (including, at least, property rights) may legitimately be infringed by the state for reasons that to a thorough-going Lockean would seem altogether insufficient to justify such infringement, but holds that there are other rights that should be reserved for special protection and so are much more constraining as to which state actions are permissible. In the United States, typical of such rights are those that are explicitly protected by the Constitution, or are said by the Supreme Court to be implicitly protected by it. These are rights that are indeed more or less sacrosanct, in that they may only be infringed for the very weightiest of reasons.

This way of handling individual rights does not require me to say anything that contradicts the more stringent Lockean view, but on the other hand, neither does it assume that the reader agrees with the Lockean view. (Indeed, though those holding the Lockean view would tend to claim that all rights are equally *constraining*—it is wrong to violate any of them—they would agree that some rights are more *important* than others in that these rights are connected with more profound and important aspects of life, and so should be taken more seriously than others.) It simply requires me to show that gun ownership belongs in the select group of rights that deserve special protection. That, of course, is what I propose to do.

Finally, before I go on, I should mention one feature of the way I will be using the method of reflective equilibrium. It is sometimes said that this method includes basing our thinking on "considered" intuitions. Mainly, what this means is that, though the method does involve presenting intuitions as reasons for some moral conclusion or another, these reasons are not raw intuitions but, rather, ones that have been subjected to the process of checking and revision I have described. In addition, I will from time to time introduce points from the common law on the grounds that these, so to speak, are intuitions that have already been "considered." Legal principles and definitions that have emerged from the process by which precedents are set into the law arise from decisions that judges make about cases in the real world—decisions that are then either taken up, dropped, or in some cases revised by other judges. They have thus been subjected to a testing process that in some ways is more rigorous than what an armchair theorist can possibly apply.

Admittedly, law and morality are not the same thing, but as you will see, legal principles can be relevant to moral discussions similar to the present one, and in my view they deserve to be taken seriously.

NOTES

1. See John Locke, *Second Treatise of Government* (Indianapolis: Hackett, 1980 [orig. pub. 1690]) , ch. 5, especially sect. 28.
2. This is how I interpret Locke's defense of the state's right to tax at Locke, *Second Treatise*, ch. 5, sect. 140. The state may coercively take away some of my money (which is what taxation is) in order to carry out its function of protecting Lockean rights. As I am interpreting his ideas here, Locke's view would then be that these coercively collected funds may *only* be used to carry out these rights-protecting functions.

3

Self-Defense

A Right that Deserves Special Protection

■ □ ■

PEOPLE WHO DOUBT THAT THERE is a right to own a gun at all may be forgiven if they wonder how on earth a thoughtful person could think it is actually not merely a right but also especially constraining on the state's right to coerce citizens. Actually, in recent years some philosophers have argued that this right is connected, closely and in a way very much to the point, with a right that most people would agree does deserve special protection: the right to use force—lethal force, if necessary—in self-defense. This idea even figured prominently in two recent Supreme Court decisions: *District of Columbia v. Heller* (2008) and *McDonald v. Chicago* (2010). In both *Heller* and *McDonald*, the court has held that there is a right to self-defense and that, as the court phrased it in *McDonald*, "this right applies to handguns."[1] If there is a right to use force, including lethal force, in self-defense, then there is a right to own guns, including handguns. This is the view that I will defend in what follows.

First, though, what about this lethal self-defense right? How can there be such a thing? Doesn't everyone have a right to life, a right that makes killing in general wrong?

As I see it, there are two principal arguments for recognizing such a self-defense right. Both can be found in the following paragraph from Locke's chapter on self-defense, which he titles, suggestively, "Of the State of War":

> The state of war is a state of enmity and destruction: and therefore declaring by word or action, not a passionate and hasty, but a sedate settled design upon another man's life, puts him in a state of war with him against whom he has declared such an intention . . . ; it being reasonable and just, I should have a right to destroy that which threatens me with destruction: for, by the fundamental law of nature, man being to be preserved as much as possible, when all cannot be preserved, the safety of the innocent is to be preferred: and one may destroy a man who makes war upon him, or has discovered an enmity to his being, for the same reason that he may kill a wolf or a lion; because such men are not under the ties of the common law of reason, have no other rule, but that of force and violence, and so may be treated as beasts of prey, those dangerous and noxious creatures, that will be sure to destroy him whenever he falls into their power.[2]

The first of the two arguments I see here is one I think of as the *distributive justice argument*. It might be expressed roughly as follows: An aggressive attack by one party upon another increases the likelihood that one party or the other will be killed or injured. Given that in this circumstance there is a guilty party (the aggressor) and an innocent one (the victim), this presents the agents in this situation with two alternatives: the increased likelihood of injury or death will fall on either the innocent party or the guilty one. Since the safety of the innocent is to be

preferred to that of the guilty, the burden here should fall on the aggressor.[3]

The other argument I have in mind, oddly tangled up with the distributive justice argument in this paragraph from Locke, is the *forfeiture/suspension argument*. Here the idea might be, again roughly, that the right to life and other rights are part of the framework of principles on the basis of which it is possible to interact with our fellow human beings on a humane and civilized basis. This is what Locke calls "the ties of the common law of reason." By violating, or undertaking to violate, the rights of an innocent victim, the aggressor is violating this framework and thus loses legitimate claim to the protection of these same principles. Locke believes that a human aggressor is like a ravening beast of prey: lethal force is legitimate in one case because one's attacker *cannot* conform his or her behavior to such rules, and in the other case because the individual *will not*. Depending on how one works out this argument in detail, the aggressor either forfeits the protection of this sustaining framework or causes it to be (as far as this interaction is concerned) suspended.

A few words might be called for to address a certain worry that might make someone balk at the notion there is a right to lethal self-defense. This is the notion that those who defend themselves against attack, or who make plans or preparations for doing so, are playing the part of "vigilantes" or "taking the law into their own hands." Such a notion confuses a profoundly important distinction. Punishment and deterrence of crime are functions of the law. *Defense* against crime—meaning by that phrase either self-defense or one agent's active defense of another— are services of a fundamentally different character. The

deterrence that is the result of punishment does afford the service of protecting individuals against crime, but this service differs from what I am calling "defense," in that the former has a feature economists attribute to "public goods": it is "non-excludable." If the legal system does a good job of punishing thieves, and thus of discouraging people from committing thefts in the future, this a considerable benefit, but for whom? The benefit falls to everyone in the area who owns anything worth stealing. Within the area of operation of the punishing authority, the system is not able to focus this benefit on some people and exclude others from it. On the other hand, defense as I am defining it here is the activity of interfering with particular individual attacks on person or property. As such, it is focused on benefiting a specific individual or specific individuals. Many economists would say that such defense is just the sort of service that ought to be offered by private agents, on the market, because if the expected benefit of such defense is greater than its costs, then the individuals who benefit from that defense will choose to bear the costs and the market will provide this service "efficiently." With public goods like deterrence, these same economists would say, private provision is much more problematic.[4]

What public policy ought to be like on this particular issue need not concern us here, but my point is that the state and its legal system *do* provide punishment and deterrence and *do not* provide defense in my sense. One court case after another has held that the police do not have a duty to protect individuals in the absence of some "special relationship" with that individual, even in cases that to a lay person would appear to be ones of gross and shocking negligence on the part of the police.[5] The duty the police have

is to protect "the public at large"—that is, to provide the public good by deterring crime. Because the level to which they provide this public good always falls short of perfection, in the sense that there will always be some crime and some consequent likelihood of suffering attack, some people will have good reason to make up some of the resulting deficit by taking defensive steps on their own. Those who take such steps are not poaching on territory that rightly belongs to the state and the law; they are doing something that the system has made very clear it has no obligation to do at all. This is just as true of those who take active defensive steps, such as hiring a bodyguard or purchasing a gun and learning to use it safely and effectively, as it is of those who take passive defensive steps, such as buying a burglar alarm system or better locks for their doors.

John Locke saw quite vividly the difference between the private function of defense and the public ones of punishment and deterrence. Shortly after the comment I quoted above, he adds this:

> Thus a thief, whom I cannot harm, but by appeal to the law, for having stolen all that I am worth, I may kill, when he sets on me to rob me but of my horse or coat; because the law, which was made for my preservation, where it cannot interpose to secure my life from present force . . ., permits me my own defense.

The reason for this stark difference—between a right to kill a thief who is only robbing me of my coat and a lack of a right to harm at all the thief who has (that is, in the past) taken all I am worth—is of course the difference between defense and punishment. In the former case, Locke is

thinking of a thief who, though he only wants your coat, is threatening you with lethal force. In that case, there is an issue—whether the thief will actually kill you or not—that will be decided before the forces of the law can possibly intervene. As a contemporary aphorism has it, when seconds matter, the cops are only minutes away. For Locke, the issue that your attacker is forcing on you places you and the aggressor in a state of nature in which civil society, for the moment, cannot help you: "force without right, upon a man's person, makes a state of war, both where there is, and is not, a common judge."[6] The reason you have a right to kill the thief is not that the thief deserves to die; it is that you have no obligation to die yourself. A state that made self-defense in such situations illegal would not be promoting law and order; it would be siding with murderers against their victims.

NOTES

1. *McDonald v. City of Chicago*, 130 S. Ct. 3020 (2010), syllabus, 4; and *District of Columbia v. Heller*, 128 S. Ct. 2783 (2008), 56–57. For philosophers who have argued for this view, see Samuel Wheeler, "Self -Defense: Rights and Coerced Risk-Acceptance," *Public Affairs Quarterly* 11, no. 4 (1997): 431–43, and "Arms as Insurance," *Public Affairs Quarterly* 13, no. 2 (1990): 111–29; Todd C. Hughes and Lester H. Hunt, "The Liberal Basis of the Right to Bear Arms," *Public Affairs Quarterly* 14, no. 1 (2000): 1–25; Samuel Wheeler, "Gun Violence and Fundamental Rights," *Criminal Justice Ethics* 20, no. 1 (2001): 19–24; Michael Huemer, "Is there a Right to Own a Gun?" *Social Theory and Practice* 29, no. 2 (2003): 297–324; Timothy Hall, "Is There a Right to Bear Arms?" *Public Affairs Quarterly* 20, no. 4 (2004): 293–312; and Lester H.

Hunt, "The Right to Arms as a Means-Right," *Public Affairs Quarterly* 25, no 2 (2011): 113–30.

2. John Locke, *Second Treatise of Government* (Indianapolis: Hackett, 1980 [orig. pub. 1690]) sect. 16.

3. For a recent version of the distributive justice argument, see Philip Montague, "Self-Defense and Choosing among Lives," *Philosophical Studies* 40 (1981): 207–19.

4. I am referring here to an enormous literature. A classic statement still often cited is Mancur Olson, *The Logic of Collective Action* (Cambridge, MA: Harvard University Press, 1965 and 1971), 9–16.

5. A fairly recent case that provoked a great deal of comment is *Warren v. District of Columbia* (444 A.2d. 1, D.C. Ct. of Ap. 1981). A woman dialed 911 when two men broke into her apartment. One patrol car rolled past the building without stopping, and an officer from another car knocked on the door and left when there was no answer. Meanwhile, a roommate of the caller was being brutally raped by the two men. Eventually, the caller and her roommates were beaten, tortured, and raped over a period of 14 hours. They sued the District of Columbia and the individual officers for damages and lost, even though it was clear the police had violated their own departmental procedures in handling the case. The legal duty of these officers to follow these rules was not a duty *to* these individual women. Wisely, the plaintiff's argument did not rely on the idea that it did; it held that by making *some* efforts to help (i.e., knocking on the door), the police had "volunteered" to help the victims, thus acquiring a special-relationship-based duty to defend them. Sadly for them, the appeals court decision rejected this argument.

6. Locke, *Second Treatise*, sect. 19.

(Easterbrook, Bauer, and Posner) was eventually reversed by the Supreme Court in *McDonald*. However, in the course of rejecting the argument of the eventually victorious plaintiffs in the case and affirming the lower court's ruling against them, the justices said something that is interesting and very much to the point at issue:

> Self-defense is a common-law gloss on criminal statutes, a defense that many states have modified by requiring people to retreat when possible, and to use non-lethal force when retreat is not possible. An obligation to avoid lethal force in self-defense might imply an obligation to use pepper spray rather than handguns.[1]

This raises the question of the extent to which possession of one right might imply an additional right against having a given means to exercise the first right taken away. Does the state violate your right of self-defense if by coercive measures it leaves you no means of self-defense other than pepper spray? The judges clearly think the answer is that it does not. But elsewhere in their written opinion they say this:

> Suppose a state were to decide that people cornered in their homes must surrender rather than fight back—in other words, that burglars should be deterred by the criminal law rather than self help. That decision would imply that no one is entitled to keep a handgun at home for self-defense, because self-defense would itself be a crime.[2]

Here they imagine, for the sake of the argument, a state that simply eliminates the right of self-defense, and what they find themselves imagining is a state that takes away every means of exercising it. This, combined with their comment about pepper spray, suggests that a right of self-defense, if it exists, would indeed place some limits on the state's power to take away the means of exercising it: the state violates an existing right of self-defense if it takes away *all* means of exercising it, but does not violate it as long as it permits *some* means of exercising it. Depending on how this is interpreted, the idea could be a rather weak constraint on state power: it could mean that a state that prohibits the use of any sort of weapon in self-defense, but allows individuals to fight off armed attackers with their bare hands, is not violating those individuals' right to self-defense.

We can imagine a standard that is weaker yet. Hugh LaFollette, in responding to an anti-restrictionist argument by Samuel Wheeler that gun bans violate the right to self-defense, makes a comment that would deem the right to self-defense an even weaker constraint on government coercion than it is in the view of Easterbrook et al.:

> [Wheeler] argues that the right to bear arms is fundamental since guns are the best way to protect our fundamental interest in self-defense. However, on his view, guns are not inherently valuable, they are valuable only as a means of self-defense. I fail to see how this could make the right to bear arms fundamental.[3]

LaFollette is relying here on a broad distinction he makes between "fundamental" rights and "derivative" rights. Fundamental rights are ones that protect a fundamental interest, where a fundamental interest is understood to be a good valued by everyone, and valued moreover by everyone as an end in itself. Derivative rights, on the other hand, are rights that either are based on some other right or that protect interests not fundamental in this sense. On this view, it is fairly clear that self-defense is a fundamental right, since people value being alive as an end in itself. However, possessing a weapon cannot be a fundamental right because people do not universally prize weapons as ends in themselves: they are at best only a means to an end. Even if there is a right to keep weapons, it would only be a derivative right. As LaFollette understands it, this claim has important policy implications, as he also holds that derivative rights are more "lax" than fundamental rights.[4] That is, it is easier (perhaps much easier) to justify abridging, suspending, or abolishing a derivative right than would be the case with a fundamental right. What is most important for my purposes is that his position clearly implies that, if the government were to take away from you every means of self-defense, it would not thereby violate your right of self-defense. You would still possess the right in pristinely unviolated condition; you would simply be unable to exercise it, rather like a citizen who has a right to vote but lacks transportation to the designated polling place on Election Day.[5]

By now we can see that there is a wide spectrum of possible solutions to the problem of whether the right to self-defense involves a right to some means of exercising it, such as gun ownership. At one end of the spectrum is the notion that the right of self-defense does not, of itself, give one a right to any means of exercising it. Then there is the thesis in the middle of the spectrum that implies one has some means, but that any means will do. At the other end of the spectrum, there is the theoretically possible extreme view that the fact that some thing is a means to exercising this right always implies that one has a right to that thing, no matter what that is. Where along this spectrum is the ideal solution to be found?

As I have suggested, this question is well worth asking because it has implications that go way beyond the ethics and jurisprudence of self-defense. The issue we are confronting here in regard to the right to self-defense arises in connection with many other rights, including some we prize very highly indeed.

For example, there are a great many rights that are rights to do or not to do certain things. I will call these "option-rights." Option-rights are rights against others that they not force us to take one particular course of action when alternative options are available. To choose one of these options is to exercise that right. The right of self-defense is an option-right. So are the right to vote, the rights to freedom of the press, freedom of religion, and freedom of speech, and the right to practice one's livelihood. For every option-right, there are means to exercise that right. For instance, various means of transportation can be used to exercise the right to vote. Similarly, churches, mosques, temples, synagogues, and other places of worship, as well as a wide array of sacred objects, are used in the exercise of freedom of religion. Printing presses and other devices for reproducing the written word are used in exercising freedom of the press, and an enormous variety of technological devices (including many sorts of electronic devices) serve in the exercise of freedom of speech. Given that there are many governmental activities—including taxation, zoning, trade regulations, safety regulations, and environmental policies—that interfere with the use of such devices, it could be worthwhile to consider when such interferences violate rights and when they do not.

Some option-rights might imply "means-rights"—that is, rights to a means of exercising those rights.[6] Means-rights, in this sense, are rights against others that they not coercively prevent one from acquiring or using some means of exercising an option-right. The broader issue before us, of which gun ownership is a sort of subissue, is this: Do option-rights indeed have this implication; and if they do, under what circumstances and why?

It is easy to see that the intuitive appeal of the more extreme positions on this issue is weak. Consider first the position that was conveyed in LaFollette's earlier comment. We might formulate it as stating that the option-right of self-defense is independent of any right one might have to possess and use any means of exercising that right; that is, an act that violates the latter right (supposing that such a right exists) does not by virtue of that fact violate the former right. Such a view is not plausible on the face of it, however. Consider the following story reported by a Fort Lauderdale, Florida, television station:

> PALMETTO BAY. Miami-Dade police put out evidence cones marking spent shell casings after a Palmetto Bay resident was shot in the parking lot of his apartment complex on June 1, 2010.
>
> John Lee says he's convinced they would have killed him if he hadn't had his gun. Lee was talking from his hospital bed Wednesday about the three armed robbers who ambushed him in the parking lot of his Palmetto Bay apartment complex, shooting him four times as he fired back with his own pistol.

"They told me 'give it up,' but they didn't give me a chance. They just shot," Lee said as he lay sedated in his Ryder Trauma Center bed. . . . Lee was set upon as he got out of his car at the Royal Coast apartment complex where he lives shortly after midnight Tuesday morning.

Lee said the bandits gave him no opportunity to comply with their demands before two of them started shooting.

"The first bullet caught me in the hand and spun me around," Lee said. "I reached for it. I started firing my gun. I must have gotten hit a couple more times, but I didn't feel it at the time. I just started firing back, and the guys ran off." . . .

Lee, a father of four and a supervisor at Sam's Club where he has worked for ten years, got a permit to carry a concealed weapon several years ago. . . .

Lee says he drew his gun, a Glock semi-automatic pistol, only after the robbers started shooting. He's convinced the attackers, who made no attempt to conceal their faces, would have killed him had he not been armed.

"If I hadn't had my gun on me, I wouldn't be talking to you right now," Lee said. "They would have finished me off."[7]

Suppose that when John Lee had pulled his gun out, someone had coercively prevented him from using it. Assume for the sake of the argument that the gun was a double-action revolver, and someone grasped the cylinder, preventing it from turning and aligning a fresh round with the barrel. Clearly, that person would have violated not merely Mr. Lee's property rights in the gun but also his right to defend himself.[8]

If that is correct, it would mean the position I have attributed to LaFollette is simply wrong. That position would imply that, in my imagined scenario, Mr. Lee's right of self-defense is not being violated at all. The position would be that, if there is any right violated in this case, it is not the right of self-defense but simply a certain property right over the gun, a right that presumably is less stringent or less important than that of self-defense. When applied to cases like that of Mr. Lee, this is not on the face of it a very plausible position.

Indeed, reflection on cases involving other option-rights readily suggests a more general truth: that any genuine option-right implies a right to *some* means of exercising that right. Obviously, a New York City ordinance prohibiting the construction of a mosque anywhere within its city limits would violate the option-right involved in Muslims' freedom of religion, even though a mosque is "only" a means to exercising that right.[9] A similar view would be true of a mob that repeatedly broke into the offices of a newspaper and destroyed its printing presses. Though the presses are only a means of exercising the option-right involved in freedom of the press, that freedom obviously implies a right not to have every such means taken away.

If that is so, what should we say about the extreme version of the principle considered by the Seventh District Court of Appeals—that the option-right of self-defense *only* rules out depriving citizens of every means? Suppose that, when Mr. Lee reaches for his gun, he finds that it is not there. His attackers have surreptitiously removed it in order to disarm him. He has no means of self-defense left other than trying to fight off the attack with his bare hands or to hide behind his car, both of which offer little hope of success. It seems that, though taking his gun away did not make him unable to perform any action at all that could be described as "self-defense," it does violate his right to

What, though, about the somewhat less easy and less obvious question raised by that court's comments: Is the option-right still unviolated if the wielder of coercion leaves some (that is, just any) means of exercising it? Let's take a first step toward answering this question by standing it on its head: Isn't the right *violated* if some—that is, just any—means is *taken away*? After all, if the state bans the use of even one category of communicative devices— all currently existing iPhones, for instance—many actions that exercise the right of self-expression will have been coercively prevented. And if the ban is really effective, actions in which people communicate via one commercial brand of smartphones will cease altogether. Why doesn't this violate the right to freedom of expression? Similarly, if the government bans the use of one class of defensive weapons, it will be cutting back on the self-defensive activities of some people. Actions in which people defend themselves by means of, say, bazookas and fragmentation grenades will have been prevented. Why does this not constitute a violation of their right of self-defense?

As I have pointed out, it is easy to think of examples of means of self-defense that do not seem to be implied in the right of self-defense. Further, this right is hardly unique among option-rights in this respect. Similar sorts of cases can be cited for other option-rights—probably for all of them. If I were to build a speaker system on the roof of my house that was powerful enough to make speeches expressing my views clearly audible over a two- or three-city-block area, that would indeed be a means of exercising my freedom of speech, but my *right* of free speech would not give me the right to do that. Again, suppose that, upon getting into my car to drive to the polling place shortly before the polls close on Election Day, I find that the car will not start. Obviously, this gives me no right to take someone else's car. I may not flag down a passing motorist and demand the car at gunpoint, even if the consequence is that I will not be able to exercise my right to vote in that election. Similarly, freedom of religion does not give anyone the right to conduct human sacrifices nor, perhaps, animal sacrifices either, for that matter.

Such examples can be multiplied indefinitely. They all seem to involve, in one way or another, a means of exercising an option-right that is either acquired or used in a way that violates the rights of others. However we might formulate the principle that specifies which means-rights follow from a given option-right, that principle must clearly include an acknowledgment of these sorts of considerations. Liberals and libertarians would probably want to express this idea by saying that an option-right cannot give someone a right to acquire or use means in ways that violate the rights of others or that harm others. Legal paternalists and legal moralists might want to define this proviso more broadly: paternalists would want to exclude means that harm the agent who acquires or uses them, and moralists would want to exclude means that are simply morally wrong, regardless of whether they harm anyone. Perhaps we can avoid this tangle by specifying that an option-right cannot give someone a right to acquire or use means in ways that involve wrongdoing, with the understanding that some moral theories hold that only certain sorts of wrongdoings are relevant here.

So, we now know one thing about the sort of principle that can help us draw the needed line between means-rights that are and are not implied in a given option-right: whatever the principle is, it must include a proviso about wrongdoing. That is, an option-right cannot give someone a right to use or acquire a means by a relevant sort of wrongdoing. That, of course, doesn't tell us which means-rights it *does* give.

Suppose that this proviso is the only limit on the means-rights generated by an option-right. Since individuals who exercise a given option-right will presumably wish to use the best means that, as a practical matter, are available to them, perhaps one principle worth considering is this:

> *The Principle of Best Means*: An option-right includes, as an essential component, a right to acquire and use the best means of exercising a right, provided this means is acquired and used without the relevant sort of wrongdoing.

In addition to the *necessary* condition on implied option-rights (one *only* has a right to means that do not violate the proviso), this principle lays down a condition it specifies as *sufficient*. According to this idea, the sovereign authority is violating a given option-right if it coercively prevents someone from acquiring or using the means to exercising it that would otherwise be the best available.

This idea might be plausible on the face of it, but I don't think it works for all cases. Consider the possibility of a nation that (unlike the United States) requires religious organizations, along with other not-for-profit organizations, to pay taxes. Resources that would otherwise go to religious purposes are diverted by the state to other uses. Some places of worship do not get additions to their buildings that would otherwise have been built. By and large, buildings are more crowded. Stained glass displays might be less awe-inspiring, and so serve a little less well as aids to contemplation. Steeples might be a little less tall. The means used for religious ends are not quite as good as they would be without the tax; thus, they are not the *best possible* means. However, though this tax policy might be objectionable on other grounds, it clearly does not violate the right to freedom of religion.

It appears that option-rights, as a general rule, do not include a right to the very best means of exercising those rights. Yet, as we have seen, it is not plausible to claim that the relevant means-right entitles someone merely to some means or other, in which case any means will do. I suggest that what it does entitle someone to is means that are *effective* for the purpose of exercising that option-right. For instance, my legs, given that both are functional, are a means of my getting to the polling place but, if the polls are hopelessly beyond walking distance, or too far to walk to in time to vote, they are not an effective means. In such circumstances, if someone coercively deprives me of all other modes of transportation, leaving me only the use of my legs, that person violates my right to vote. This sort of consideration explains why not just any means will do. For example, fighting with your bare hands is a means of self-defense, but as I have pointed out, if Mr. Lee had been deprived of every other means, he would not have been able to actually defend himself. The same is true of means like pepper spray or using his car as a shield.

A means of doing a particular type of action is effective, let's say, only if it affords the agent a substantial assurance of achieving the goal that is internal to that action-type. The internal goal of an action-type is one that is mentioned or implied in any proper definition of that type of action. Alternatively, one can think of the internal goal as a goal necessarily ascribed to an agent whenever someone regards that agent as performing or attempting that type of action. In this sense, the internal goal of voting is successfully casting a vote. A person who is engaged in the act of voting may also have any number of other purposes—fulfilling a civic duty, impressing his neighbors, magically causing one candidate to win, and so on—but the mere fact that the person is voting necessarily means that the individual intends, by so doing, to get that action recorded and counted in the relevant way. Only someone who has this goal can truly be said to be voting (rather than, say, performing some sort of ceremony that involves going through the same physical motions). The internal goal of self-defense, thus, is thwarting attacks against oneself and thus avoiding violent injury and death resulting from such attacks. If I am undertaking to defend myself, this is what I am necessarily trying to achieve. Thus, we have the following way of drawing the needed line:

> *The Principle of Effective Means*: An option-right includes, as an essential component, a right to acquire and use an effective means of exercising it (provided this means is acquired and used without the relevant sort of wrongdoing), where "effective means" is understood as a means that affords the agent a substantial assurance of achieving the goal that is internal to the action-type that the option-right entitles one to perform or, failing that, comes as close to that level of assurance as can be achieved.

Clearly, the qualification at the end of this statement— about the highest achievable level of assurance—is needed.

The reason is that for some actions with an internal end, there is simply no way to ensure that this end will be achieved. Indeed, some enterprises fall desperately short of that that sort of certainty. In such cases, it would be absurd to deny that the agent has a right to the best of those imperfect means that remain. In that event, the Principle of Effective Means is equivalent—in terms of what means it requires as a right—to the Principle of Best Means.

This point is a very important one for attempts at self-defense, which so often fall into this category of uncertain and even desperate undertakings. In this way, they are typically different from attempts to cast a vote, which can often be assured of success by means that are simple and easily carried out. For transportation to my own polling place, which happens to be a church at the other end of a bicycle path, my own legs suffice. Typically, similar things are true of the right to freedom of religion. The internal goal of the acts to which this option-right entitles one is to practice one's religion (or no religion at all, if one so chooses). For this, fairly rudimentary means typically suffice. Even if you worship in a cramped and ugly temple, you have still succeeded in worshiping.

With self-defense, on the other hand, matters are quite different. The end that is internal to self-defense, as I have said, is to thwart or deter attacks—and more particularly, to avoid death, injury, and other losses inflicted by such attacks. There are unfortunately a great many situations in which such an enterprise cannot be substantially assured of success. This means that, under the Principle of Effective Means, the option-right includes the right to acquire means that come as close as possible to ensuring success (provided this is done without relevant wrongdoing). This, of course, would be the best means available (subject to the same proviso).

This conclusion raises rather obviously the question of what constitutes the best means. It is, on the face of it, extremely plausible that the best means in many cases (though of course not in all) is a handgun. There are other, more ancient means of self-defense—such as skilled use of various pointed or sharp-edged weapons, or hand-to-hand martial arts—that can be remarkably effective in specific circumstances; but it is common knowledge that, while such methods are effective in various circumstances, they require years of study and, in many cases, innate talent or physical strength. Handguns, on the other hand, are effective in an enormous variety of situations. For instance, they are useful in very close quarters (unlike long guns), though (unlike knives and pepper spray) they do not *require* someone's target to be very close. This is a factor that was important in Mr. Lee's case. The needed skills, and the all-important safety rules, are easy to learn and can be mastered by any adult of normal intelligence who has the use of one intact hand.

Obviously, the claim that something is an effective means to do something is an empirical claim: it is a claim about the world based on experience and observation of some sort. Does this mean that we need scientific empirical studies to make such a claim? Clearly, such studies do not seem necessary to back up at least a crucial part of this claim. The reason for this lies in the nature of the claim that something is an effective means. Such a claim signifies that this instrumentality affords an agent with a substantial assurance of achieving the goal that is internal to that act-type. That is, the means is effective in the context of a particular act. We do not need empirical studies or sophisticated statistical methods to know, for instance, that automobiles and one's own legs are, in particular circumstances, effective means of getting to the polls and thus of exercising one's right to vote—nor, for that matter, that bicycles and roller skates are also effective means. Similarly, we do not need such sophisticated evidence to know that in particular circumstances a gun can be an effective means of self-defense. This seems to me a matter of ordinary common sense. This is also a situation in which anecdotal evidence, such as the incidents reported in Chris Bird's recent book *Thank God I Had a Gun: True Stories of Self-Defense* can be pertinent and compelling,[2] .

Of course, one could plausibly argue that to say a given measure violates the Principle of Effective Means goes beyond claims like these and involves the further assertion that the measure violates the underlying option-right by preventing completion of the relevant act. This raises the potentially thorny issue of whether, to make such a claim true, it is sufficient that the measure has this effect in one case, or whether a substantial number of cases must be affected in this way in order to say the measure violates rights. Frankly, it seems to me that common sense and anecdotal evidence are, again, sufficient to support this assertion—that is, that interference that prevents one person from completing the act thereby violates the rights of that one person—, although I realize there can be honest disagreement about this.

What does the empirical literature have to say about this issue? There is one sort of statistic that, despite its appearing frequently in the literature, can be dismissed as irrelevant. We often see factoids like the one produced by a team of four doctors who studied accident and homicide figures from 1958 to 1973 in one county in Ohio. They found that there were 148 fatal gun accidents (78 percent of them in the home) and only 23 burglars and other home invaders killed by armed residents. Thus, they reasoned, a gun is six times as likely to kill its owner or a family member in the home as to kill a criminal trespasser. Their conclusion was that "the possession of firearms appears to be a dangerous and ineffective means of self-protection."[3]

I find this argument strange. To be meaningful and to the point, it has to be about two things: how much damage can be expected that a gun will do and how much good it can do. The "good" in this case consists of how many lives are saved, injuries are averted, and property loss is avoided. Now, admittedly, it is not easy to measure these events. Measuring things like numbers of lives saved means measuring the rate at which something doesn't happen but otherwise would have happened if not for some allegedly life-saving device. It isn't easy to count things that almost happen.

What we need is some proxy variable that can stand in for this measurement in some meaningful way. The above argument assumes that the number of intruders killed by residents is such a stand-in. Indeed, we sometimes see statistics like this quoted by people who equate the number of defensive gun uses (DGUs) with the number of people *killed* by would-be victims of crime. Of course, those numbers are not the same, and the latter is not a good indicator of the former. There are several studies of how often guns are used defensively, but they all report that the number of defensive uses is far greater than the number of lethal uses. In itself, the number of lethal defensive uses tells us nothing about the value that a defensive use of a gun has. The point of legitimate defensive action is not to exterminate the "bad guys" but to defend the rights of victims. In itself, the taking of a human life is always a regrettable event, even if a necessary one. Without some formula for determining the relationship between the number of fatal shootings and the number of defensive uses, the result is as meaningless as a numerator without its denominator.

There is, of course, a body of research that deserves to be taken seriously on the actual rate of DGUs on the part of civilians. In this research, the most common approach is to use answers that people give to survey questions as the proxy variable. For example, people in a sample group are asked whether in the last year (or ever, or over some other period of time) they have used a gun to protect themselves (or their property, or anyone else) against a crime or an attempted crime. Then the researchers (or others using their data) extrapolate from those to generalizations about the population of the whole nation.

Alas, to date the studies using this method have arrived at a bewildering variety of results. At one extreme is an ambitious survey conducted in 1993 by Florida State University criminologist Gary Kleck and his colleagues. Their sample population was 4,977 adults living in the lower forty-eight states in homes with telephones. Based on 222 completed interviews with respondents who reported DGUs the preceding year, Kleck and his colleagues estimated that there are between 2.2 and 2.5 million such incidents nationwide each year.[4] At the other extreme, as far as results are concerned, are various studies that use data collected by the National Crime Victimization Survey (NCVS), which is carried out by the U.S. Department of Justice.

A typical result derived from this source is 116,000 DGUs per year, or about 5 percent of the Kleck estimate.[5] What is particularly baffling is that the NCVS does not seem to use methods dramatically different from the Kleck study.

One thing that both sides seem to agree on is that these numbers have major policy implications. One research team using the NCVS figures has drawn the conclusion that "armed self-defense is extremely uncommon."[6] Although it would be difficult to prove this, there seems to be a preponderance of opinion that the NCVS number, if correct, would weigh heavily against the self-defense case for firearms ownership. In defense of his results, Kleck has pointed out that another large survey, conducted by Philip J. Cook, his principal critic during the 1990s, produced an estimate of DGUs per annum that was also far in excess of the NCVS data; according to Kleck, Cook's number amounted to 1.5 million. (Kleck also claimed that NCVS's raw data actually justifies a larger estimate of 2.73 million.) In addition, writing in the summer of 2000, Kleck indicated that there were nineteen relevant surveys and that *all* supported substantially higher estimates of DGU rates than did the NCVS, the latter being the only survey to report fewer than 700,000 annual DGUs.[7]

The NCVS does seem to be the outlier on this issue. And yet it has, and deserves, great respect in the scholarly community. Being a project of the federal government, it is better financed and uses a larger sample population that the other surveys, as well as being repeated annually. Further, the NCVS consistently produces what Kleck refers to as "deviant" results. What could account for this fact? Kleck cites two general sorts of factors that could explain those results—ones that support higher DGU estimates without impugning the integrity of the NCVS. First, since the survey is not designed specifically to investigate DGUs (but, rather, victimization), it does not specifically ask about these incidents. Instead, it asks whether the respondent has ever been the victim of a crime; and if the answer is yes, there is the follow-up question, "Was there anything you did or tried to do about the incident while it was going on?" The respondent is then allowed to volunteer that he or she used a gun. Events that are not specifically asked about in the surveys are consistently underreported in them.[8] Indeed, the order of these two questions would tend to eliminate completely *successful* acts of self-defense, in which the would-be criminal is fended off or scared away, with no damage done. Also, non-expert respondents might not reflect that attempted rape, robbery, and the like are themselves crimes, and this may lead to an excess of "no" answers to the first question, thus to cases in which the follow-up question is never asked.

More important, while respondents in surveys about gun use are assured of their anonymity, the respondents in the NCVS are aware from the beginning that they are not anonymous. The interview begins with the interviewer's taking the respondent's name, address, and contact information, as well as the names of everyone in the household. The respondent is also told that the interviewer represents the Department of Justice, which is the enforcement arm of the federal government.[9] Now, there are obvious reasons why someone who has pulled a gun on a fellow citizen may hesitate to talk about it under these circumstances, and those reasons go well beyond "paranoid" concerns about the government's future use of this information to confiscate guns (but see chapter 8, below).

Laws concerning firearms are complex and often poorly understood. This is true of the legal rights and wrongs of owning and carrying them as well as those of threatening someone with one or firing at them. There are jurisdictions where it is unlawful to carry a legal weapon outside of one's home, and a great many where it is illegal to carry a concealed weapon without a proper permit. Thus, even just having a gun in the place where an incident occurred could, in many cases, be an offense of some sort, let alone using that gun or threatening someone with it. Even civilians with a DGU to report who are *pretty* sure that what they did is in every respect legal may well feel sufficiently insecure to be hesitant to tell a representative of law enforcement about the incident. In these circumstances, we should expect such incidents to be seriously underreported.

These considerations seem sufficient to indicate that the NCVS-based estimates of DGUs differ from the others because they are underestimates. The sensible assumption is that guns are used for self-defense significantly more often than these estimates suggest.

It is perhaps obvious by now how the Principle of Effective Means, together with the considerations that support it, satisfies the three desiderata I set out earlier: the need to justify, or at least explain, three intuitively appealing notions. If the case I have made for the Principle of Effective Means is sound, all three of these notions are indeed true.

I have earlier suggested a response to the third desideratum, which is that of explaining or justifying the idea that an option-right does not generate means-rights to every means of exercising that right. To be more precise, I have suggested justifications for the idea that there are two sets of means to which option-rights might not confer means-rights. One set of cases is covered by the wrongdoing proviso; here, all the cases I discussed are behaviors that violate the rights of others. A possible justification for the proviso, which is available to libertarians and perhaps liberals as well, would be to argue that that an option-right—not only the right of self-defense but other option-rights as well—cannot entitle one to violate the rights of others. People who prefer a broader, moralistic, or paternalistic interpretation of the proviso might be able to construct similar sorts of justifications.

The other set of cases has to do with the fact that the Principle of Effective means only grants a right to effective means, not to all means nor even to all non-rights-violating means. In those cases in which (as is typically the case with the right to vote) the effective means of exercising an option-right falls short of the best means possible, none of the (even-)better means is included in the right. A law that prohibits some powerful methods of transportation (perhaps because they unduly pollute the atmosphere) would not thereby violate someone's right to vote if the remaining means are effective for this purpose. After all, the fact that the remaining means are effective means that the law is not coercively preventing anyone from voting.

Some of the considerations that led to the Principle of Effective Means provide us with a response to the second desideratum: they justify the proposition that the relationship between the action that violates a right and the action that (merely) takes away the means of exercising it seems to be identity. As I have said, option-rights are rights to do certain actions, and all actions that have internal ends consist of using means that effectively enable one to do them. It follows that one of the ways in which one can coercively prevent the action from being done is to interfere coercively with someone's access to such effective means. But to coercively prevent the action from being done *is* to violate the option-right. Thus, coercively taking away the effective means is (identical to) violating the option-right. The basis of the explanation of the identity desideratum, then, is the same in kind as that of the answer to the "easy question" raised by the Seventh District Court of Appeal's comments: the basis is the nature of purposive action itself. This also, rather obviously, explains the equal stringency desideratum: it justifies our intuition that the ("mere") means-right sometimes can be as stringent as the corresponding option-right. Two rights are equally stringent in this sense if violations of them are wrong in equally serious ways. Violations of means-rights are wrong in ways that are just as serious as violations of option-rights, simply because they *are* violations of option-rights.

If my discussion of the Principle of Effective Means and the three desiderata sounds to you like a hair-splitting treatment of matters that are really verbal and not about reality, consider how it applies to a real-world example. During the primary election campaigns leading up to the 2016 U.S. presidential elections, there were news reports that two terrorists who had murdered fourteen people in San Bernardino, California, had discussed their violent jihadist views on Facebook and other social media. Donald Trump, a candidate for the Republican nomination, responded by saying in interviews that we should consider "closing that Internet up"—at least "portions" of it.[10] Critics swiftly pointed out that if this is not a targeted measure aimed at specific criminal activity, then it would be unconstitutional. What they meant, of course, is that it would violate the right of free speech.

This is exactly what my view implies. Such a measure would not merely limit the means of exercising the right; it would violate the right itself. Further, this is a truth about the relationship between means-rights and option-rights in general, and ultimately about the nature of the actions they are rights to do. And it applies to the right to own a gun as much as it applies to the right to own a working Internet connection. A government that disrupts the Internet is violating the right to free speech, and one that disarms its citizens is violating the right to self-defense.

NOTES

1. (1) and (2) are somewhat clearer statements of claims Todd Hughes and I made in "The Liberal Basis of the Right to Bear Arms," *Public Affairs Quarterly* 14, no. 1 (2000): 8.
2. See ch. 1, n. 7. The National Rifle Association maintains a web page, "Armed Citizen," that features true stories, generally from local press reports, of private citizens who have used guns to prevent or interfere with a crime. Typically, they run several new stories each week; see https://www.nraila.org/gun-laws/armed-citizen.aspx.
3. See Norman B. Rushforth, Amasa B. Ford, Charles S. Hirsch, Nancy M. Rushforth, and Lester Adelson, "Violent Death in a Metropolitan County: Changing Patterns in Homicide (1958-74)," *New England Journal of Medicine* 297 (1977): 504–505. Gary Kleck points out that the authors unknowingly inflate the accidental death numbers by including the total number of accidental deaths in their numerator, rather than the 78% that occur in the home. Gary Kleck and Don B. Kates, *Armed: New Perspectives on Gun Control* (Amherst, NY: Prometheus, 2001), 311.

More damningly, he points out that the same journal published another study a decade later, in this case by Arthur L. Kellerman and Donald T. Reay, that used the same sort of logic, though with a different set of data, and that the second study not only does not mention the first, but also shows no awareness of the criticisms that had been leveled at the first one (312).

4. Kleck and Kates, *Armed: New Perspectives*, 215–25.
5. David McDowall, Colin Loftin, and Stanley Presser, "Measuring Civilian Firearm Use: A Methodological Experiment," *Journal of Quantitative Criminology* 16 (2000): 4. This is the number that the NCVS collected for the year 1993–1994, approximately the same time as the Kleck survey.
6. David McDowall and Brian Wiersma, "The Incidence of Defensive Firearms Use," *American Journal of Public Health* 84 (1994): 1984.
7. Kleck and Kates, *Armed: New Perspectives*, 226–29.
8. Ibid., 229–30.
9. Ibid., 232–33. Elsewhere, Kleck and a co-author point out that in in-person interviews, the interviewer commences by displaying an ID card and badge. Gary Kleck and Marc Gertz, "Armed Resistance to Crime: The Prevalence and Nature of Self-Defense with a Gun," *Journal of Criminal Law and Criminology* 86, no. 1 (1996): 154.
10. Commentator Wolf Blitzer questioned him about his comments in the fifth Republican debate of the season. A transcript can be found at https://www.washingtonpost.com/news/the-fix/wp/2015/12/15/who-said-what-and-what-it-meant-the-fifth-gop-debate-annotated/.

6

The Ethics and
Jurisprudence of Risk

■ □ ■

ONE WINTER DAY SOME YEARS ago I was driving with my teenage son on the freeway from Oregon, Wisconsin, to Madison. We entered a dense fog. I could only see about thirty feet in any direction; beyond that, everything was a solid gray murk. I had slowed down radically. Suddenly a car whizzed past me, going at least 65 miles per hour. I said to my son, "Gee, Nat, if there is a semi jackknifed across the road ahead, that stupid jerk is going to plow right into it. There's just no way he could stop in time in this fog!" Sure enough, news reports began to emerge a few hours later of an incident on Interstate 90 nearby. Some drivers entered the fog and slowed down to the proper speed. They were rear-ended by a semitrailer truck that had not slowed down. There followed a series of crashes that grew hideously into a 100-car pileup. It blocked both sides of the freeway and stretched for five miles down the road. One person said that cars kept coming in "like rockets." Police estimated that some of the cars involved must have been going 70 miles per hour when they slammed into their victims. It is perhaps lucky that only two people were killed, but about fifty went to the hospital.

What shocked me about this was the very thing that amazed me even before the disaster happened: so many people were driving as if it were a normal day. Why didn't more people notice that they couldn't see a damn thing, and drive accordingly? The political scientist Aaron Wildavsky once made a distinction that I believe is useful for explaining phenomena like this one—a distinction between the two "broadest strategic alternatives for attempting to secure safety."[1] He called those alternatives "resilience" and "anticipation." A resilient system spots errors and modifies itself accordingly. An anticipatory system aims to predict errors and avoid them. Trial-and-error is a resilient principle. Anticipation aims at trial without error.

Rightly or wrongly, most drivers on a highway are usually in a state of mind that relies on resilience. As far as their conscious thoughts are concerned, they wait for something to go wrong; perhaps the driver ahead of them is going so slow that they will collide if nothing changes, at which time they notice it and alter their behavior to repair the situation. For instance, they might either change lanes or slow down. It is debatable whether resilience is really a good strategy for driving on a highway under normal conditions. However, it is lethally disastrous when driving in a dense fog. The behavior of the drivers who flew into the fog bank like rockets was wrong, but not as irrational as it might seem at first. They were driving as they usually do on the Interstate, prepared to change if something were to go wrong. They simply had not switched from resilience to anticipation soon enough.

It is important to realize that neither of these strategies is, in general, wrong. Resilience is often a good strategy; in fact, it characterizes the state of mind most of us are usually in. The rocketing drivers were simply practicing resilience at the wrong place and wrong time. In our lives we use both sorts of strategy, sometimes simultaneously. But sometimes we tend to rely more heavily on one strategy, and at other times more on the other. To use anticipation for all hazards would be far beyond the capacities of the human brain. A person who is constantly in a state of anticipation would be in dire need of psychotherapy. It would mean constantly thinking about everything at the same time. In everyday life, we usually rely on resilience as the default, background response to risk, shifting into anticipation when it is called for.

Modern societies use both strategies. The deterrence function of punishment is a case of anticipation: it is an attempt to suppress (deter) possible future "errors" (crimes) that would otherwise occur. On the other hand, tort law is a resilient system. Once an error, such as an injury caused by negligence, happens, the process seeks a "remedy" (the legal term that is used), which typically is monetary damages awarded to the wrongly hurt plaintiff. The award of damages is not meant to deter future infractions, but to fix one that has already happened.

In the English Common Law countries, such as the United States, the tort law system also contains another, more profound sort of resilience. In deciding cases, judges follow precedent where it is applicable. This means relying on solutions reached for problems that have already happened. Precedent is closely related to another sort of resilient system: tradition. Tradition is a clear example of a resilient system, at least if it remains adaptable and does not petrify. A living system of traditions is an evolving response to the problems of life as they have actually occurred.

The issue of state responses to risk brings us back to unfinished business from Chapter 5. To put the issue in terms of my example of Mr. Lee's encounter with his assailants: Though I haven't said it in so many words, I have been proceeding as if the Principle of Effective Means implies that Mr. Lee had a perfect right to possess and use his Glock semi-auto in the way he did. After all, we know with the clarity of hindsight that his attempt at self-defense ended without further injury to himself, and it is doubtful under the circumstances that any means of self-defense that fell short of the power, accuracy, and medium-range effectiveness of a handgun could have had any hope of success.

But this is only part of what the principle requires. There is also the proviso about wrongdoing. This condition of no wrongdoing is not special to issues of self-defense and lethal means; it is one that should be attached to any right whatsoever. To deny this proviso would seem to commit us to the notion that someone can have a right to violate the rights of others. But what relevant sort of wrongdoing might Mr. Lee be guilty of? His response seems to satisfy the classic conditions for justified self-defense. It seems to have been a necessary response to an attack that was unlawful and under way, and his reaction was not out of proportion to the nature of the threat. Any room for debate about this would belong to the intricacies of the ethics of self-defense. Such issues need not concern us here, being a matter for another book. However, there is one matter that I do need to discuss. Mr. Lee has a gun, after all, and guns are dangerous objects. Is there a chance that this means he is wrongfully exposing his fellow citizens to risk of injury and death?

This brings us close to the core of the rationale for gun control. Restrictive gun legislation seems to be a pure case of Wildavskian anticipation. Even punishment, which I have used as an example of anticipation, nevertheless has an obvious component of resilience: it is a response to an injury, homicide, or other offense that has occurred. Restrictive gun legislation is a *pure* attempt prevent events that would violate people's rights if they were to happen – namely, being injured or killed by gunfire – *which have not happened*. The rationale is to coercively remove the means by which such rights-violating events might happen.

The first thing to say about this sort of rationale is that most people—and indeed, our legal system—treat some cases of anticipatory coercion as entirely legitimate. For example, I may not store dynamite in my basement, nor may I drive while intoxicated. No doubt part of the reason for this is that if my car were to hit somebody, or if my store of explosives were to turn my neighborhood into a smoking crater, these events would violate the rights of other people. I am prohibited from doing these things even when no such damage or injury has been done.

The notion that *coercion can be justified on the grounds that the actions prohibited subject others to risk*—what might be called the Principle of Risk—is eminently plausible. This principle—which might more accurately be called the risk-to-others principle—is particularly plausible if we note that it is very different from the paternalistic risk-to-self principle. We are not talking about forcing people to stop doing actions by which they put themselves in danger—things like smoking, eating the wrong foods, and failing to use seatbelts or motorcycle helmets. The issue here is one of imposing risks on others.

Even within the context of imposing risk on others, there is a large and difficult question about what *sorts* of risks can justifiably be thwarted by coercive means.[2] After all, even tort law, let alone criminal law, does not always coercively intervene, even in cases of harm that is *actually caused*. If Mr. Lee were to harm someone with his gun, he theoretically could try to claim the "defense of due care," invoking the principle that a person can ordinarily only be forced to pay damages for injury that he caused by acting *negligently*. That is, even actually causing damage is not necessarily grounds for coercively imposed liability.

However, there is another sort of risk, other than negligence, that tort law singles out for coercive interference. This is when part of the reason for that interference is the *nature* of the risk to which the injured party was exposed. We can learn something interesting about the ethics of risk management by pausing to consider this particular basis for coercive interference by the state. This is the sort of risk involved in what the law often calls "inherently dangerous" or "ultra-hazardous activities." If injury to life, limb, or property resulted from such an activity, the plaintiff can collect damages without having to prove that the defendant was negligent: due care is no defense. This is usually known as "strict liability."

Lists of such ultra-hazardous activities, in cases cited in standard textbooks, might include the following: blasting with high explosives, keeping a chimpanzee (which injured an invited guest), keeping a horse known to be vicious (which kicked an unoffending neighbor), impounding a large reservoir of water (which leaked and damaged a neighbor's coal mine), and pile driving (which produced vibrations that damaged neighboring property), using hydrocyanic acid gas to kill cockroaches in a building with other tenants, launching rockets to test rocket fuels, crop dusting, drilling for oil (which can produce unpredictable explosions), and transporting gasoline in tanker trucks on public highways.[3] What do these actions have in common? As the relevant legal decisions have stated many times, all are instances of actions that (1) are not commonly done, (2) necessarily involve a substantial risk of serious harm to others, and (3) cannot be made safe even with the exercise of utmost care.

Why do you suppose the law singles out people who engage in such hazardous activities, subjecting them to a burden (strict liability) to which others who do risky activities are not subject? Clearly, condition (3) is crucial. Each of the listed actions involves, in some sense, the unleashing of natural forces—the pressure of many tons of water contained by layers of soil, the whims of a vicious horse, drifting clouds of crop-duster poison—and these forces *cannot* be controlled with precision by human effort. There is no such thing as doing these things in a completely safe manner.

There is a problem here, though. Each of the activities listed above promises some social benefit, but a disproportionately large share of that benefit is expected to go to the agents (corporate or individual) that carry out or decide to carry out these activities. At the same time, as these activities are carried out, they necessarily impose risk on unconsenting people in the area. In some cases, it is a substantial and deadly risk for many people over a large area. This seems a clearly unjust distribution of benefits and burdens. How to rectify the situation? The legal solution, which began with a mid-nineteenth-century decision in the British House of Lords, and has evolved over decades of cases, is to permit the activity but compel those responsible for it to pay full damages, denying them defense of due care.[4]

Like most of the legal doctrines that are arrived at in this scrupulous, incremental way, this seems an eminently wise solution to a real problem. It is true that it inflicts a certain level of coercive interference on an activity, allowing it but imposing strict liability, but there is an intuitively appealing justification for doing so. This justification—for this particular level of coercive interference, which falls far short of prohibiting the activity—clearly does *not* apply to owning or using a firearm, however. The reason is that owning or using a gun fails completely to satisfy condition (3), which is crucial for an activity's being "ultra-hazardous." Owning and using firearms are actions that *can* be done in a completely safe manner. Consequently, as counterintuitive as this might sound to some, these actions do not, as such, impose any risk on people other than the responsible agents.

Though guns are obviously dangerous objects, they represent a far different—in fact, virtually the opposite—sort of hazard from the above-listed ultra-hazardous activities. Whereas there is no way to control precisely which way the rocks will fly when a charge of dynamite is detonated, the precise control of the flight of a bullet is, in a sense, the entire purpose of a gun. Unlike automobiles, fireworks, and most other dangerous objects, modern guns are precision instruments. In fact, marksmanship, which is one of the hobbies based on gun ownership, consists very simply in perfecting and enjoying this precision as an end in itself.

There are three simple safety rules that, in one version or another, have been repeated in in countless gun-safety courses and are well known to responsible users everywhere: (1) Keep the safety (if applicable) in the "on" position until ready to use; (2) Keep your finger off the trigger until ready to shoot; (3) Keep the muzzle pointed in the safest direction (which usually is downward). Following simple rules like these makes it impossible to injure someone unintentionally. The same sort of thing cannot be said of injuries caused by sticks of dynamite or clouds of poisonous dust.

Further, possession and use of firearms can enhance the safety and reduce the risk to people in the area. In fact, they very often do so. I have a friend whom I will call Clifford. Clifford is a professor of a humanistic subject and the author of many books. He is also a lifelong firearms hobbyist and owns many guns. Indeed, they are all over his house. He and his wife raised their half-dozen children, not by childproofing their guns but by the more labor-intensive (and some experts say, ultimately safer) approach of gun-proofing their kids: by teaching them as early as possible to respect guns and to take them utterly, completely seriously.[5] When Clifford is out of the house, he typically—unless he knows he will be in an establishment that does not allow it—has a loaded handgun concealed somewhere on his torso. He also frequently has a "second chance" weapon—a knife or a smaller gun—in one of his boots. I guess this makes him what many people call a "gun nut." Yet there is really nothing that is "nuts" about him. He is an utterly competent, responsible, and rational human being. He simply has a different ethical outlook and a different array of interests from the typical humanities professor. It no is doubt partly due to such factors that I feel safer, less at risk, when I am with Clifford (and know that he is "carrying") than when I am without him.

How is such a thing possible, given that guns are considered dangerous? Part the answer to this question lies in the nature of risk. Risk is a phenomenon of probability in which, as the mathematicians would say, the probability involved is in the interval between 0 and 1. If I know there is something out there that is sure to kill me, it is not something that puts me at risk; I am simply doomed and I know it. Risk, on the other hand, is linked to uncertainty. Risk is, thus, like life itself, which always involves uncertainty of one sort or another.

When I am with Clifford, I am never completely certain exactly what will happen next, anymore than I am during the rest of my time on earth. The fact that his weapons are deadly, especially in his capable hands, is part of my on-balance estimate of the situation. This in a way is precisely the point: his hands, the man who owns them, and the fact that the relevant estimate is on balance. I know that in the event (admittedly unlikely) that we should suffer a violent confrontation, he would consider it his duty to defend not only himself and his family but also all other innocent life, including mine. I also know that he is a competent and knowledgeable user of these weapons. Thus, the net risk effect of his weapons on me and other innocent human beings is not to increase risk but to reduce it. Further, it is perfectly rational of me to see the matter this way.

In case this sounds like an odd thing to say, just consider that this is the way many people view a certain enormous collection of handguns that exist in the world today. I have in mind the guns in the hands of local, state, and national police forces. We see the police as enhancing our safety on balance and, though we usually have little reason to reflect consciously about it, we surely see their weapons as making a powerful contribution to this effect. As with the effect Clifford's weapons have on my security, this view is compatible with viewing these guns as highly engineered, impeccably crafted instruments of death and destruction. Indeed, their (potential) destructiveness is an essential element in our positive on-balance estimate of their effect on risk and safety.

This is an important conceptual point. As I have said, risk—and indeed, its opposite, which is safety or security—is a phenomenon of probability. It is also a global phenomenon. That is, risk is a relatively large-scale fact that includes other, relatively "local" facts as constituent parts. The effect of Clifford's weapons on my security is global, while the fearsome destructive potential of his weapons is a local effect in relation to it. Note that the global phenomenon is not seen, heard, or felt but, rather, is discerned by the rational mind by means of what I have called an "estimate." On the other hand, fear—that spasm we feel on contemplating the gun in Clifford's waistband—is resolutely local.

This curious feature of fear was pointed out decades ago by Robert Nozick.[6] He proposed a thought experiment in which we imagine two different scenarios. In the first, person X hears that person Y, having had an accident and broken his arm, was later compensated with $2,000. X thinks this is adequate compensation: it covers the injury. In the second scenario, Z tells X that, some time in the next month he will break X's arm and then pay him

$2,000. X spends the whole month as a nervous wreck. He is apparently *not* indifferent to the combination of broken arm plus $2,000: in some way, the $2,000 fails to cover the injury. Do we think that X is being inconsistent? No. There is one big and relevant difference between the two scenarios. In the second, X knows in advance that he will be injured, and so he has a chance to experience fear of the impending future event. That fear attaches to the event and refuses to be swallowed up by X's estimate of the larger, injury-plus-compensation estimate of the situation.

This effect does not disappear even if we were to double or triple the compensation. There are reasons for this epistemic tenacity of fear (I would even argue that it is characteristic of emotions in general)[7] The tinge of fear in someone's perceptions of the destructiveness of guns—a destructiveness that is ear-splittingly obvious to any-one who shoots on an indoor firing range—helps us stay mindful of their power and consequently be better able to handle guns safely and to the advantage of the innocent. But it can also lead to illusory estimates, as when we think of them *simply* as "dangerous," where this means that the mere fact of their destructive potential constitutes a net risk that owners and carriers of guns impose on others. It is our fear of the potential of guns that makes it feel as if this were so.

Returning to the question of whether the state is justi-fied in coercing Mr. Lee because of the risk he wrongfully imposes on others, consider this: If we suppose that the rel-evant "others" must be innocent others, the answer seems to be no, it is not justified. The simple reason is that in Mr. Lee's case such risk does not exist. Or, better, it exists but it is negative. Mr. Lee's having this gun transformed what would have been a virtually hopeless situation into one in which he had a fighting chance—and actually, as it turned out, he survived. Thus, his firearm figured in his situation as a risk-reducing, safety-enhancing factor.

However, the pro-restrictionist is not about to run out of replies at this point. Hugh LaFollette, and many others, would say that my question about Mr. Lee is the wrong question, mainly because it *is* about Mr. Lee and his *specific* circumstances. As LaFollette puts it: "[G]un control does not concern what private individuals should do but what governments should permit private individuals to do. We must determine the risk of permitting the private owner-ship of guns."[8]

Framing the question in this way means taking the issue of the management of risk in a way that contrasts with the one I am taking here in two important ways. First, it frames the issue as one of justifying permitting the individual to do something. This places the burden of proof on the individual who, in effect, is seen as beseeching the state to allow him or her to do something, rather than requiring the government to justify interfering. No doubt, what motivates this way of framing the issue is the notion that after all guns are dangerous and, for instance, by pos-sessing a gun Mr. Lee is imposing risk on innocent others. This would be a defensible approach if instead of possess-ing a gun he were proposing to drill for oil. There is no way to drill a shaft to an unknown depth into a reservoir of flammable fluids under an unknown, possibly enormous amount of pressure in a safe way. In that case, he would be exposing others in the area to risk simply by doing the activity. Depending perhaps on how we might settle other questions (how big is the "area" affected by the risk and are there really any people in it? is the level of risk high enough to matter? should we consider the value of this activity to the rest of society?) it might be right that the burden of proof should fall to showing that the activity should be permitted. But of course I have argued that the activities of owning and even carrying a gun are not like this at all.

Having said that, I should admit that there is a deeper issue here, one that I have not discussed yet. It concerns different types of risk. Surely, there is such a thing as the general level, within a given geographical area, of the risk that a given individual will be violently killed or injured. Since guns are instruments by means of which people can be injured or killed, this raises the possibility that the sovereign authority can significantly reduce this risk by simply refusing to permit private ownership of guns. It also raises the possibility that it can also reduce this sort of risk by restrictionist regulation that falls short of outright prohibition. The sort of risk we are imagining here is, we might say, imposed on the general population by a group of people: those who own or carry guns. It varies completely independently of the behavior of any particular individual or corporate body. If there is a sort of risk that increases or diminishes because a given group of people increases or diminishes in size, then it seems that it would indeed be risk that is imposed by a *group*. Let us call this sort of risk, the sort that is imposed by a group of people, type-risk. The contrasting sort, which is imposed by particular agents (including corporate bodies) I will call token-risk. The sort of risk I have been discussing so far, the sort that Mr. Lee does not seem to be imposing on any innocent people, is token-risk. He nonetheless is a member of a group of people that, as a group, might be imposing a quite different sort of risk on innocent others. Can this sort of risk, type-risk, be a legitimate ground for coercively interfering with him?

Type-risk is a profoundly different sort of reason for interference from token-risk. It is also, clearly, a much weaker one, for at least two reasons.

First, the habit of treating type-risk as a legitimate ground for coercion does not seem to be a feature of the moral point of view that is typical of people who live in liberal democracies such as the United States. At least in the United States, people typically see things from the point of view that can roughly and intuitively be described as *individualism*. On this view, moral discourse is about individuals: it is about how individuals are responsible for what they do and ought to be *held* responsible for the consequences of their actions. Most important, individuals can be held responsible for treating the rights of other individuals with respect.

Within the individualist moral point of view, what heightened type-risk "really" means is that there are irresponsible or downright evil individuals who are violating the rights of others. On this view, coercing Mr. Lee for a reason like this, leaving him in effect defenseless against his attackers, is "punishing" (or penalizing) him for the actions of others. Such a policy is simply wrong, except perhaps in circumstances of catastrophic social collapse, such as widespread mob violence. Obviously, we do not live under such conditions now. Admittedly, some moral philosophers do not agree with individualism; in particular, utilitarians do not. My point here, however, is that type-risk is a weak reason for coercion, in that it has little or no purchase within the individualist community, which includes most citizens of liberal democracies who have not been convinced by philosophical theories like utilitarianism. Of course, one can still present it as a reason nonetheless, but in that case one should be prepared to make some sort of theoretical argument for non-individualist moral reasoning.

Second, recall the proviso that was written into the Principle of Effective Means. Would it make sense to consider preventing type-risk as part of this proviso? Even supposing that the prevention of type-risk does belong in our moral point of view as a legitimate ground for coercion, this would be the wrong way to incorporate it. To see why, consider an example I used in an earlier chapter: smartphones, tablets, and other Internet communication devices. Everyone is aware of people who use such devices while driving, and has heard claims that this "distracted driving" causes accidents. Suppose for the sake of the argument that the government can significantly reduce accidental injury and death by shutting down such communications on the part of civilians, reserving their use for the military, police, and various other agents of the state. (It might help, to simplify the issues involved, to imagine that they have a way of doing this without shutting down devices, such as desktop and laptop computers, that are not typically used while driving.) Suppose also that by simply going after individuals who deserve to be penalized, like actual distracted drivers, they cannot bring about a like savings of life and limb. We would be denied these means of communication, while all around us government messages would me swarming through the ether. But we would have that substantial saving in life and limb to console us, as the justification for this interference with our way of life.

Obviously, the government would nonetheless not institute such a policy simply for such a reason as this.

Imagine the uproar if they tried it! Of course, there would be many reasons for that storm of outrage, but clearly one would be the feeling that our rights to communicate with fellow human beings had been violated. Clearly, the Principle of Effective Means, apart from the proviso, implies that we would be right in feeling this way. There would be uncountably many messages that could not be sent due to this coercive interference on the part of the state.

But what about the proviso? It recognizes that individual rights are limited by the like rights of others: whatever else might be included in a right, it cannot include the right to violate the rights of others. Though a ban on mobile communications devices would reduce type-risk, as we are assuming for the sake of the argument, it does not mean that any single individual is violating the rights of others. It is perfectly consistent with the fact that, as would no doubt be true, some individuals would be calling for help for other people who have been injured in accidents or calling to report the erratic behavior of unsafe drivers—that is, it is consistent with the fact that some people would be using their mobile devices to *enhance* the safety of others. As far as type-risk is concerned, such facts make no decisive difference. Type-risk is a global, all-things-considered sort of consideration. Such risk-reducing behavior is just one sort of consideration. These would-be helpers are still, by our assumptions, members of a *group* that imposes risk on others.

But why *not* include such global considerations in the proviso? Isn't that the real issue here? The shortest and most confident answer I can give is that such a move would represent a profound change in the way most of us think about rights. Notice that the proviso is not about how individuals should employ a given right but, rather, about whether they have the right at all. To include such global considerations as type-risk in our moral theory at this point would mean that there could be a right that then ceases to exist in the event the state can achieve some policy goal by acting as if it did not exist. Admittedly, this is how modern states tend to treat certain rights (property rights being an example of rights singled out for this sort of treatment), but in the liberal democracies we set aside a class of rights for special protection *precisely* because we do not want those rights to be sacrificed in this way to the greater social good.

For example, there is one important reason we recognize a right to freedom of speech, even when someone is communicating bad or even dangerous ideas. We do not even bother to do studies of whether we are safer when people are allowed to defend communism, fascism, racism, and other socially destructive ideas. The right to communicate ideas is insulated from greater-good, public policy sorts of exceptions.[9] The same is true of freedom of religion. More generally, there are no legitimate policy-based exceptions for these important individual rights. If that is so, then surely this general point applies to the right of self-defense, which the Principle of Effective Means serves merely to explicate.

Have I proved that this general point is true? Of course not. This is an essay in philosophy, and as far as philosophy is concerned, liberal democracies could be altogether mistaken in isolating a class of rights that is special in this way. But I have said enough to show that the strategy of denying this general principle, or of denying that it applies to self-defense, would be a revision of our basic moral conceptual scheme. This means that the burden of proof rests on those who wish to make that revision.

I must admit, though, that LaFollette's way of framing the issue raises a whole nest of issues in the gun control debate that I have not begun to address. Or perhaps it is more accurate to say that it is a way of describing the issue that captures an important pro-restrictionist theme I have yet to touch upon. Notice that LaFollette said that the real issue is about "what governments should permit private individuals to do." We need to determine, he says, the risks of permitting such a thing. Just now I was discussing an issue concerning the right of the individual who is subjected to state authority. In LaFollette's statement, the issue is framed as a moral problem for the sovereign authority itself. Don't states have not merely a right but also a duty to consider the risk of permitting citizens to do various things? As with most duties, which are simply the other side of a right, this does imply a question about rights, but a different one than I have considered so far: don't citizens have a right, a right *against the government*, that it do something about such generalized levels of risk? Don't sovereigns have a duty to provide for public safety and don't citizens have a right to such provision?

The most immediately plausible answer to both questions, of course, is yes. But there are many ways of defining exactly what this answer means, and some of those ways make all the difference for the issue of gun control. For instance, most anti-restrictionists would agree that the state has both a right and a duty to punish, deter, or exact compensation from individuals who wrongly impose risk on unconsenting others. But this obviously is token-risk, and that is not what we are contemplating here as a possible ground for coercion. Here, we are talking about type-risk. This fact brings into the foreground an important feature of this notion of the rights of the state. This notion is functionally equivalent to the revision of the proviso, which we were just considering, that is based on the same sort of risk. That is, if either notion justifies coercive interference with individual behavior, then both justify exactly the same interferences. There is, however, one big difference. What the revision of the proviso means is that, for reasons of policy, certain individual rights cease to exist. The notion of the rights of the state does not have this implication. As far as that is concerned, the individual rights that we are ignoring when, say, we confiscate Mr. Lee's weapon might nonetheless exist. We would in that case simply be violating those rights.

Looking away from the issue of individual rights and focusing instead on the rights of the state makes individual rights momentarily invisible, but that does not mean they cease to exist. One is either assuming that reasons of policy can justify state actions in violating individual rights, or that they imply such rights do not exist when they get in the way of relevant state policies (i.e., the same point that the revised proviso implies). In either case, the burden of proof is on those who would invoke the alleged right of the state to reduce type-risk by means that coerce unoffending individuals.

There is another aspect of this claim of a right on the part of the state that I should say something about before moving on. As I have pointed out, the state's right would seem to imply a corresponding subject's right. Should we agree that there is such a right? Notice that this is a right of a very particular sort. The state already reduces our risk—or

equivalently, enhances our safety—by a vast array of coercive moves against individuals, groups, and corporate bodies that violate the rights of others. For instance, the state
deters crime by punishing those who harm us in life, limb,
or property. It takes coercive measures against those who,
in breach of contract or the legal duty of due care, subject
us to unsafe buildings, faulty consumer products, hazardous driving habits, and so forth. The idea we are now enter-
taining holds that we have a general right against the state
to be made safe, even aside from such measures as these. If,
after the state has done all these things, life still falls short
of the level of safety to which we are alledgedly entitled,
then we have a right to state action to make up that deficit.
Presumably, this would have to include coercive measures
against people who are not violating the rights of others.

I see several large problems with the notion that there
is such a right. The first might be obvious by now, so I will
be brief about it. It is the problematic nature of coercing
those who are not violating the rights of others. The right
to be safe, if it exists, is a "positive right," like the rights to
an education or to medical insurance. That is, it is a right
to be supplied with something (at the expense of others,
if need be). The problem is that, regardless of what positive rights you might believe in, everyone who approaches
social issues in terms of rights agrees that we also have
"negative rights." These are rights against others that they
not do certain things to us. That is, negative rights are constraints, limiting the methods that may legitimately be
used to pursue one's goals, including the goal of providing
people with those things that come with positive rights.
All the rights mentioned in the American Bill of Rights
are negative rights—rights that constrain state action.

In contrast, positive rights are often treated as if they automatically justify states in doing whatever they deem necessary to pursue the goals involved. They do not carry this justification automatically, however. People's negative rights include a right of self-defense, certain resulting means-rights, and some presumption against being molested by the state when one is innocent of an offense against others. If a right to safety is to justify restritionist moves against individuals, some argument must be given why this right overrides the negative rights that are being ignored or violated in the process. Typically, no such argument is given.

So far, I have been assuming, for the sake of the argument, that there is a relevant right to safety. I see two major reasons for denying that there is. First, such a right would be hopelessly vague—far more vague than any legitimate right has any reason to be. As mentioned earlier, when measured on the risk scale, a person's safety is always between 0 and 1. A person is always under some finite probability of death or other harm, whether it is from sudden heart attack, developing cancer cells, being hit by a car, or being blown up by a terrorist. Furthermore, between the 0 and the 1, there are infinitely many possible degrees of risk and safety. Thus, there is no such thing as simply *being safe*; one is always subject to risk, and always to a certain degree of it.

Consequently, there is no such thing as, simply, the government's making us safe. It must always take specific steps and achieve some definite level of safety. If the government has a duty to make up the deficit in safety left over from its other, obviously legitimate measures, then one must answer this question: How much safety am I entitled to? The vague notion of a right to be safe does not even come close to answering this question. It looks like a good reason for a specific restrictionist regulation only to those who are already convinced on other grounds that the regulation is justified.

In this respect, the alleged right to be safe is different from other positive rights, such as the rights to education or health insurance. Unlike schooling and insurance, a safe(r) environment is a public good: it is nonexcludable, consumed by the public at large. Proponents of these other positive rights are not committed to saying that there is a right to a specific amount of the goods involved: they are only committed to making them available to those who have a right to them. Public safety is not like that.

The second reason for denying a general right to be safe is related to the first. Given that the level of safety varies continuously and is never perfect, more safety is always available, but at ever greater cost. This complicates the issue of determining the right level of safety by introducing the question of what safety level is worth its cost. People differ enormously in how much cost they are willing to absorb for a given increment of security, where "cost" means whatever is being given up or forsaken to get it. We see this in the different degrees to which people indulge in or avoid foods, drinks, and drugs they know will increase their risk of diabetes, heart attack, cancer, or a multitude of other dangers. We see it in the various types of insurance policies people purchase or avoid purchasing. Even if someone buys insurance, there are choices made regarding deductibles and coverage levels. Did you insure that expensive new bicycle you just bought? Or is it already covered by your homeowner's insurance? Did you bother to check?

I used to embarrass my classes by asking students if they buckle their seatbelts when they ride in a car. Most answered that they did not. It is tempting to think of such personal failures to take safety steps as simply irrational and to label all risk-averse behavior as prudent, but I think this is wrong. People are simply different. Not only do we have different degrees of risk aversion, but we have different responses to different kinds of risk. Some people are more worried about being the victim of a crime, while others, even when circumstances are similar, are more concerned about heart disease or cancer. In this regard, remember that where crime victimization is concerned, we are *not* talking about whether the state should deal coercively with those who violate the rights of others or subject them to the risk thereof. Even if all crimes and other offenses have been dealt with, there are additional safety increments for those who consider the extra cost worthwhile. They may install burglar alarms, put bars on their windows, or purchase a gun and master its safe and effective use. Given that added security costs something, and that people rationally and legitimately strike different balances between levels of safety and the costs of obtaining them, how can a given level of security be a right? Because the level of safety that the state supplies is a public good, such a right would also be a duty to take the same package deal as everyone else is getting.

There is one more reason to resist the notion that there is a right to a general level of risk that is worth discussing here. It is slightly different from the one I have just given, but closely related to it. A right to a general level of risk tends to carry an arbitrarily bias toward anticipation and away from resilience in one's policy preference regarding the state's handling of risk. It would seem that a certain leaning toward either resilience or anticipation as one's preferred strategy is one of the legitimate, purely personal ways people differ from one another. Some people are content to deal with problems as they arise, while others prefer to head them off before they happen. If one thinks of the risk of bad things happening as somehow a matter of rights, it is natural to look at risks as simply being unacceptable. After all, violations of rights are unacceptable, aren't they? This, therefore, implies a strategy of anticipation.

I believe a certain a bias toward anticipation rather than resilience bolsters the plausibility that gun restrictionism has for many people, while at the same time deeply dividing them from anti-restrictionists. As I have pointed out, gun control is an extreme example of anticipation. When our son was old enough to crawl around the house and get into trouble, my wife and I covered all power outlets and stowed all dangerous substances in places that were out of reach, or in bottles that a child could not pry open, or in cabinets with special latches that a small child cannot puzzle out how to unlatch. We did not want to spend his first several years trying to pound safety rules into his head, given that he was not yet able to understand these rules and follow them himself. Better to simply make it impossible for him to cause accidents! Similarly, gun restrictionism aims to make "gun violence" impossible, or at least less possible. The basic idea is the same, except the environment is a nation-state, not a house, and the people we are attempting to control are, for the most part, normal, responsible adults, not children. To anti-restrictionists, this view seems an objectionable, "nanny-state" policy.

NOTES

1. Aaron Wildavsky, *Searching for Safety* (New Brunswick, NJ: Transaction, 1988). 11.

2. Undergraduate student Alexander Schaeffer has pointed out to me that most of the problems that I am about to discuss—as to how to specify the Principle of Risk—would not exist in a system in which everything is private property (as in the radical libertarian and anarcho-capitalist theories we were discussing at the time). If I am in the shopping mall and behaving in a way that others find menacing, a representative of the owners, probably an armed guard on their staff, would simply escort me out. It would not matter whether the risk I pose is reasonable, unreasonable, or purely imaginary. If the owners or their authorized agents do not like what I am doing, I am out. In some contexts, the thorny ethical and jurisprudential problems of risk might be largely an artifact of contingent property relationships, not a problem posed (much less solved) by pure practical reason.

3. Victor Prosser, William Wade, and John Schwartz, *Torts: Cases and Materials* (New York: Foundation Pressy, 1976) .

4. *Rylands v. Fletcher*, House of Lords, L.R. 3 H.L. 330 (1868). Note that strict liability for ultra-hazardous activities still leaves the responsible agent with the possibility of other defenses against liability, other than due care. This is relevant to an issue raised by LaFollette (see ch. 1, n. 1). He recommends that gun owners be subjected to something he calls "strict liability" for any damage done by their guns (280–81), but what he means by that phrase is very different from what the law means. LaFollette means that one should be liable for any damage ever done by one's gun, regardless of the context and regardless of one's role (if any) in causing the damage. Under this rule, someone would be liable if his gun is stolen by a burglar, who then unlawfully sells it to another criminal, who in turn unlawfully injures someone else. This would mean that there is no proximate-cause defense against the legal strict liability rule, a defense that at present the law does allow as valid.

5. On gun-proofing, see Massad F. Ayoob, *Gunproof your Children!* (Concord, NH: Police Bookshelf, 1986) . Ayoob reaffirms his recommendations on this point in his more recent *Gun Safety in the Home* (Iola, WI: Krause, 2014), 73.

6. Robert Nozick, *Anarchy, State, and Utopia* (Cambridge, MA: Harvard University Press, 1974), 66.

7. On the "local" nature of emotion in general, see my *Anarchy, State, and Utopia: An Advanced Guide* (New York, NY: Wiley, 2015), 95–96.

8. Hugh LaFollette, "Gun Control" *Ethics* 110 (January 2000): 270.

9. In his eloquent opinion in the Hudnut pornography censorship case, Judge Frank Easterbrook points out that policy considerations of public safety were presented as strong arguments for all the major attempts at press censorship in American history, from the Alien and Sedition Acts to efforts to silence the communists in the 1950. For all people knew at the time, these proscribed ideas really were dangerous, and very seriously so. See *American Booksellers Inc. v. Hudnut*, 771 F.2d 323 7th Cir. Ct. (1985).

7

Philosophizing
About Empirical Studies

■ □ ■

I TELL STUDENTS IN MY Contemporary Moral Issues class that empirical, professionally collected evidence is relevant to some of the issues we will discuss. For instance, one topic is whether pornography is wrong in a way that might justify the state's either banning it or using coercion to restrict its availability. One factor that is arguably relevant to this issue is whether the wide availability of pornography in our culture increases or decreases the rate at which women are subjected to the crime of rape. There is an ample body of scientific writing on this subject. I assure them, though, that if there is an issue that can now be settled once and for all by such scientific studies, we would not be discussing it in our course. Proponents of positions on different sides of the issue find that there are studies they can quote to support their side. If you intend to seriously evaluate the relevant literature, you must be ready to dive in and get your hands dirty, weighing the relative merits of or disambiguating seemingly conflicting evidence and pondering different methodologies. (People who arrive at different conclusions sometimes do, not surprisingly, use contrasting methods in reaching them.) I have neither the expertise nor the space to carry out such a project here, but I would like to make some general observations about this relevant literature and offer some guidelines for thinking effectively about it.

To some extent, the fact that features of the empirical literature can be used to support one side or another of a debate is a sign of progress. Over the years, serious scholars who discuss public policy issues adapt their positions so that they do not conflict with known facts. This results in a certain tendency for the opinions of respectable scholars to become more moderate as time goes by. A few years ago, I organized a panel discussion on gun control for the annual meeting of the American Philosophical Association. I went out of my way to make as sure as I could to have two pro-restrictionist and two anti-restrictionist speakers on the four-person panel. When the speakers came to give their talks, though, the differences between their positions were so subtle that when we published our proceedings and as panel moderator I wrote an epilogue to the discussion, my contribution was titled "Is There Still an Issue Here?"[1] I did find a point about which our speakers disagreed, but I had to dig to locate it. That issue turned on matters of philosophical and legal principle, and not on matters of fact.

This suggests a more fundamental point. It is that the philosophical aspects of an issue can illuminatingly be seen as prior to the empirical ones. Admittedly, the words *philosophical* and *philosophy* are vague and are contested, even (especially?) by academic philosophers, but they have familiar meanings in ordinary language. I am thinking of usages like "I see that you are conserving our drinking water so that we do not run out before returning to base camp, but I have a different philosophy about that: we should keep up our strength now" or "The screenwriter resigned from the project over philosophical differences with the film's producers." For my purposes, this ordinary usage does well enough. What my more fundamental point means is that the significance of the empirical facts, the implications they have for policy issues, even which facts one possesses and how one collected them, depend on the principles, concepts, models, and metaphors one is using when considering the issue. By the time you have arrived at the facts you bring to bear on the issue, you have already made a choice between the paths that diverged, like those in Robert Frost's forest—and that, in the words of the poet, "has made all the difference."

All this is wonderfully illustrated by a rather curious feature of the scholarly literature on guns, which is that the literature on the subject that can be found in medical journals is an intellectual monoculture: it is uniformly restrictionist in its point of view.[2] If a policy-relevant article on guns appears in a medical journal such as the *Journal of the American Medical Association* or the *New England Journal of Medicine*, it is virtually certain to be pro-control in its intended implications. On the other hand, if we turn from empirical studies conducted by doctors to ones done by criminologists or lawyers, we see a great deal more diversity in point of view. Scholars on the anti-restrictionist side of the issue have long complained of the one-sidedness of the medical literature, of its extreme reluctance to refute in any detail respectable work that contradicts pro-restrictionist conclusions, or in some cases even acknowledge that such respectable work exists.[3]

A prominent anti-restrictionist scholar, Don B. Kates, claims that these features of the medical literature violate the "normal standards of scholarly discourse and even of scholarly integrity," which require painstaking sifting of all relevant evidence. He also has an explanation for these same features. This literature, he says, is "consistently result-oriented," meaning that it is driven by "an emotional bias in favor of reaching anti-gun results."[4] Such a bias would indeed be a violation of scholarly integrity.

I see an alternative possible explanation, or at least the beginnings of one; it is an explanation that is more charitable but might explain the same facts. As I understand it, this medical literature is based on the idea that guns are a public health issue. They kill and injure people. This would be difficult to deny. After all, this is (among other things) what they are designed to do. Given this way of framing the issue, it is natural to think that all the factors to be investigated by empirical researchers involve the harm that guns do: how they do it (accident, crime, suicide), at what rate they do it, and so forth. In this respect, a comment by Dr. Katherine Christoffel, an early contributor to this literature, is telling: "Guns," she says, "are a virus that must be eradicated. . . . They are causing an epidemic of death by gunshot, which should be treated like any epidemic—you get rid of the virus."[5] Kates might object that claiming guns are a virus is a metaphor and thus only reveals the emotional bias of the speaker. Indeed, this is a metaphor— it is obvious that guns are not literally a virus, or any other sort of pathogen—but it does not follow that the significance of the claim can only be emotional. Metaphors serve cognitive functions as well as emotional ones. If guns do cause harm to human bodies, then they are *like* a virus; and if they are sufficiently and relevantly like a virus, then the metaphor might serve the cognitive function of organizing the data and raising questions for future research.

Of course, once one comes under the influence of such a guiding metaphor, this can result in behavior that, to an outsider, looks as if driven by mere emotion. The failure to process information favorable to the opposing side might appear to be the result of what Kates calls "gun-aversive dyslexia," an emotional revulsion for guns that is so strong a person is honestly unable to comprehend evidence for their positive social effects.[6] But this habit of mind can have a cognitive explanation, rather than (or in addition to) this emotional one. If one thinks of guns simply as a cause of harm, it is hard to take seriously the other side of the issue—or the idea that there *is* another side. Do pathogenic viruses have defenders? And if they do, will we bother to carefully examine their arguments?

Of course, my little explanation must be developed considerably before it can explain very much. After all, there are many benign viruses, and a trained medical researcher can entertain the possibility that even a pathogenic virus might have, on balance, beneficial effects on its host. For reasons that will be clear momentarily, I will call the above-described view of guns (minus the virus metaphor) the "deterministic model." This is the idea that guns cause harms—injuries and death—to people. It is the idea that guns are the cause of these harms. If we have good reason to think that this feature of the situation is sufficiently important, it might be reasonable to encapsulate this model in the metaphor of guns as a virus or some other sort of pathogen. But the pathogen metaphor goes beyond the deterministic model by further focusing our attention and, among other important cognitive effects, directing our attention away from factors that are not worth investigating. Metaphors can be cognitively useful economizing devices; metaphors, and imagistic thinking in general, can focus the mind on important factors picked out by more abstract, less emotional sorts of thinking, such as what I am here calling a "model."

I realize there are any number of things that are strange about what I have just said. How can the idea that guns cause these injuries be a "model" at all? Isn't it obviously true? Well, it is also true to say that, as I was awakened this morning by a beeping sound near my head, my alarm clock woke me up. But this is not the only way to look at that event. It is also true that, given that I set the alarm last night, I used the clock to wake myself up. Both these statements are true, in that both correspond to the facts. Yet, in another way, the difference between them is enormous. You might say they organize the facts differently.

When it comes to alarm clocks, we all look at them (except in that foggy moment of waking up) in a nondeterministic way, which I will call "voluntaristic." That is, we think of it as a technological device used by purpose-driven agents to achieve some goal. Guns, in contrast to alarm clocks, are devices that we can easily think of either deterministically or voluntaristically. In a case like this, to adopt one model or the other is to decide that the model picks out what is really important in the situation. We encapsulate a model in powerful metaphors or other images that serve to shunt the less important factors into the background murk. Unlike the deterministic model of guns, which was crafted mainly by modern intellectuals, the voluntaristic one is embedded in American culture;

and as a result, the encapsulating metaphors are far more complex, rich, and beguiling: they reach well beyond the boundaries of a metaphor (in the literal sense of that word) into vast realms of symbol and myth. This glittering realm includes the guns of cowboys of the American West and the fictional cops and robbers of our cities. Indeed, its symbolic world is way more vast than that, as our psychologically potent imagery makes little distinction between these weapons and the arrows, spears, swords, and crossbows of those mythic heroes and villains of all the ages.

That the anti-restrictionist thinking is influenced by cultural myths is obvious to the restrictionists—a fact they make obvious when their rhetoric associates anti-control stances with a "cowboy mentality." There is much truth in this accusation. My point here is just that thinking rooted in myth is not necessarily irrational. The power of myth derives from its embodiment of fundamental concepts and principles, including those that are employed in the theories of scientists and philosophers. As my use of "voluntaristic" suggests, the concepts central to this model and the cultural metaphors that embody it include above all that of individual choice, as well as such closely related concepts as responsibility and moral character.

A research project that illustrates the voluntaristic model—one that illuminates some of its basic logic—forms the basis of economist John Lott's book *More Guns, Less Crime*.[7] Collecting data from every county in the United States, Lott studied crime rates before and after the passage of laws expanding the rights of law-abiding citizens to carry concealed handguns. Lott found that passage of such laws resulted in a broad *reduction* in the incidence of violent crime, including a 2.2 percent reduction in murder, a 3.9 percent reduction in rape, and a 4.9 percent reduction in robbery. This is *after* he controlled (via a statistical method known as regression analysis) for the effects of various other factors (such as use of capital punishment and "broken windows" policing policies) *and* in spite of the fact that the rate of some of these crimes was increasing at the time that these laws were passed.[8]

Why would this be? We cannot go far in answering this question without leaving the realm of hard fact and indulging in speculation, but one thing is fairly clear: despite the eye-catching title of Lott's book, the factor he was studying is not the quantity of guns in the population (i.e., "more guns"), but something more like their distribution. Nearly all these concealed-carry laws place a limit on who may receive a permit to do so, requiring that (details vary among jurisdictions) one not have a relevant criminal record. Whatever the effect these laws might have on the quantity of guns in society, it seems they inevitably have an effect on the rate at which a certain group uses them in a certain way, presumably for self-protection. People often seem to think of Lott's research (encouraged by the book's title) as showing that guns are good. More accurately, it presents evidence that a certain use of guns by a certain sort of person—namely, a law-abiding civilian—has a good result.

The subject matter of this research project is just the sort of thing that the voluntaristic model indicates we ought to be studying: it is not a study of the effects of gun technology as an impersonal force but, rather, of human agents using that technology to achieve their purposes. The deterministic and voluntaristic models both influence which facts researchers look for and which they expect to find.[9] They also serve as guides in interpreting and evaluating the data gathered. After all, statistical generalizations are quite different, logically, from any recommendations that follow. The gap between these two quite different sorts of ideas is filled with concepts and principles, and it is in this gap that the two models have a role to play.

It is plain that, in the conduct of everyday life, people rely heavily on the voluntaristic model. It also seems reasonable for them to do so. Consider the general sort of statistic I presented in chapter 5—the kinds of studies that show owning a gun, carrying a gun, or using a gun for self-protection is associated, statistically, with some bad effect. This is a deterministic model type of consideration. Now, what would it mean for a given individual to base a decision as to whether to, say, own a gun for protection on such a statistic? It would mean forecasting your own future, not on the basis of what you know about your own intentions, character, skill level, and so on, but on the idea that this tool, which you might decide to use, is *a gun*. Is this how a rational person makes such a decision? Or would that rational person consider the facts about him or herself— the sort of consideration the voluntaristic model pushes into the foreground—as decisive?

Perhaps the best way to get a solid grasp on this issue is to think about it with reference to a single statistic, one that often figures in pro-restrictionist research: the rate at which people commit suicide with a gun. It is a little-appreciated fact that suicides by firearm far outnumber homicides by firearm in the United States, and this has been the case consistently for as long as the Centers for Disease Control (CDC) has collected such data (i.e., since

myself. There may be a teenager who suffers from relevant psychological problems or some other person I have reason to regard as unstable. This sort of consideration expands the circle of people for whom the gun-suicide link could be relevant. Yet even for them, this factor need not be decisive. They can consider possible security devices and other means for keeping a loaded gun out of the reach of unstable individuals. The gun-suicide link, thus, seems irrelevant to the rational decision-making of a large portion of our population.

There are three points in the foregoing discussion that need to be emphasized. First, all the thinking I attribute to rational agents is in regard to individuals—their decisions, character, and so forth. This is voluntaristic-model thinking. Second, a rational agent does apply deterministic-model thinking to certain agents. If there were an at-risk teenager in my house, I would be concerned about the possibility that the presence of a gun in the house might cause a suicide on his part, in the sense that a successful attempt at suicide would happen, and would not have happened in the absence of that gun. Third, applying the deterministic model to an individual becomes rational on the basis of an imputation of *weakness*. We think of people as being led to do things by technological devices such as guns when we have reason to think of them as incapable of the responsible choices and actions that, for the most part, characterize mature persons.

Readers who are not familiar with the scholarly and polemical literature on guns are likely to think of deaths by firearm as deliberate homicides. It may come as a surprise that restrictionist authors often quietly include suicides in this group. As we have seen, doing so can nearly triple the number of "gun deaths." Anti-restrictionists often respond indignantly to this move. To them, this seems like cheating—a sort of lying with statistics. How can the deaths of people who want to die represent the same social problem as the unwilling deaths of those who are cruelly slaughtered by others?

I would say that this is not necessarily the cynical move that anti-restrictionists often take it to be. In fact, it makes perfect sense if (perhaps only if) one views it under the influence of the deterministic model. In that case, these deaths are not the results of responsible actions, and as such they are not to be weighed in accordance with our estimate—as good or evil, wise or foolish, or merely tragic—of the human wills that gave rise to them. They are mere events, alike in being regrettable and in being caused by the same brute piece of technology. In such a case, the people involved are mere parts of a causal mechanism. Yet this perhaps is a deeper reason for indignation on the part of those who do not share this deterministic vision. To look at human beings this way seems to deny them the respect and dignity due them as responsible persons.

NOTES

1. Hugh LaFollette, Lance Stell, Samuel Wheeler, Cynthia Stark, and Lester Hunt, "Symposium on Gun Control," *Criminal Justice Ethics* 20, no. 1 (Winter-Spring 2001): 40–45.
2. William J. Vizzard comments on the remarkable ideological uniformity of the medical journal literature on guns in his very even-handed discussion of the gun control issue, *Shots in the Dark: The Policy, Politics, and Symbolism of Gun Control* (Lanham, MD: Rowman and Littlefield, 2000), 9–10. Brian

Doherty discusses it as well in his "You Know Less than You Think About Guns," *Reason* 47, no. 9 (February 2016): 36–37.

3. See Don B. Kates's contribution, "Guns and Public Health: Epidemic of Violence, or Pandemic of Propaganda?" in Gary Kleck and Don B. Kates, *Armed: New Perspectives on Gun Control* (Amherst, NY: Prometheus, 2001), 31–106. This chapter is a revised and updated version of a longer and earlier paper with the same title that Kates co-authored with Henry E. Schaffer, John K. Lattimer, Edwin H. Cassem, and George B. Murray, *Tennessee Law Review* 61 (1994): 513–96.

4. Kates, "Guns and Public Health," 44 and 49.

5. Katherine Christoffel, interview in *American Medical News* 3 (January 1994): 9.

6. Kates, "Guns and Public Health," 34ff.

7. John R. Lott Jr., *More Guns, Less Crime: Understanding Crime and Gun Control Laws*, 3rd ed. (Chicago: University of Chicago Press, 2010).

8. Ibid., 171–75.

9. I think this might explain a feature of anti-restrictionist literature that one occasionally sees, which is statements like "most [murderers] would be considered law-abiding citizens prior to pulling the trigger" and "most shootings are not committed by felons or mentally ill people, but are acts of passion that are committed using a handgun that is owned for home protection." See Don B. Kates, Introduction, in Gary Kleck and Don B. Kates, *Armed: New Perspectives on Gun Control* (Amherst, NY: Prometheus, 2001), 20–21 and associated footnotes. Against this, Kates cites an array of studies "dating back to the 1890s" that show that "in almost every case murderers are aberrants exhibiting life histories of violence, crime psychopathology, substance abuse, and other dangerous behaviors" (20–21). Kates explains the contrary opinion in the restrictionist literature on the grounds that it would explain how gun control is supposed to reduce the homicide rate even though we might not expect murderers to be any more inclined to obey gun regulations than laws against homicide, the explanation being that many

murders are committed by ordinary citizens. In other words, it is a specimen of a sort of wishful thinking. But there is a more charitable explanation: it is just what one would sincerely expect to be true if one's thinking is dominated by the deterministic model: people commit "gun violence" mainly because of the guns, not mainly because of their character as individuals.

10. Pew Research Center, "Suicides Account for Most Gun Deaths," http://www.pewresearch.org/fact-tank/2013/05/24/suicides-account-for-most-gun-deaths/. Retrieved 8/30/15. Doherty, "You Know Less," 35.

11. Gary Kleck, *Targeting Guns* (New York: Aldine, 1997), 49–50. Surveying all the original studies that had been done at the time, Kleck found that of the 11 studies, 9 found no significant connection between rate of gun ownership and suicide rate, one found a positive connection (guns cause suicide), and one produced mixed results. They did find a positive correlation with *firearm* suicide (more guns causes more gun suicides) but not with suicide in general. Kleck concluded that people who are denied one means of committing suicide will substitute others.

8

Policy Implications

■ □ ■

IN LATE 2007, MY FATHER died in his home in Santa Rosa, California, leaving behind, along with other things much more valuable, several guns he had used for sporting purposes. Among them was an old Smith & Wesson .38 revolver, similar to many police service weapons used in old movies. I was surprised to find that my brother had contacted the Sonoma County Sheriff's Department, which has a program to collect and destroy guns in the hands of civilians. They gave the distinct impression in their interactions with him that they were not merely willing, but positively eager to get their hands on those old guns. (They assured him that by the time they were done with them "those guns will never shoot again," as if he should find this information soothing.) I said I wanted the revolver. It had a certain sentimental value for me. When I was a boy, Dad and my brother and I used it for shark fishing (to make sure these dangerous creatures were dead before hauling them into our small fishing boat). I also figured it would be cheaper to ship it, legally, to my home in Oregon, Wisconsin, than it would be to purchase a gun.

It turned out that, to get the gun to me, my brother had to ship it from a gun store more than twenty miles away from Santa Rosa, to a gun store that was over thirty miles from my home. This was the most convenient route permitted by federal law, which requires guns shipped interstate to go only from one federally licensed gun dealer to another. Owing to local ordinances as they stood at the time, there were no such dealers near either of us. When the gun arrived, the fees due were surprisingly large. I no longer have a record of the exact amount paid, but I do remember noticing at the time that I could probably have bought a similar used gun locally for a like amount and avoided all this trouble.

It seemed clear to me that I was dealing with regulations intended to discourage the shipment of guns between states, even when this means shipping something that is already one's own property to oneself. The net effect of these rules was such as one would expect if one were shipping explosives or caustic chemicals. Yet there was nothing in the shipping box that was hazardous in this way; there was no ammunition or gunpowder, so there was no danger it would explode.

I now realize that I should not have been surprised by this. There is a vast array of programs and rules, state, local, and federal, that range from noncoercive ones like the sheriff department's gun disposal program, to a bewildering mass of measures that involve coercion in one way or another—programs and rules that affect citizens' access to firearms. This obviously includes the local ordinances in Santa Rosa, California, and Madison, Wisconsin, prohibiting any gun dealers within city limits, as well as federal restrictions on shipping firearms. Arguments that justify such regulations have to justify restricted access to firearms on the part of competent adults. This makes such regulations restrictionist legislation or, in my sense of the words, "gun control." The argument I have offered here is that these regulations and all similar legislation are illegitimate and unjustified. They are wrong for the same reason and in the same way that rules that coercively impede people's access to the Internet or to places of worship would be wrong.

In case it is necessary to repeat myself, this argument is subject to the proviso discussed in chapter 5, a constraint that applies equally to all rights. That is, the position I have taken is compatible with laws that prohibit acts that violate the rights of others. Arguably, this means that my position is compatible with reasonable safety regulations on firearm design. It is compatible with such regulations if the features they prohibit would otherwise allow individuals who own and use such weapons to wrongfully subject others to risk (as described in chapter 6, this is token-risk). One can realistically imagine a range of possible regulations that could be defended on such grounds. This is not an interesting point, though, as such regulations are on the books and nobody is agitating to have them removed. The most I can claim here, as a possbly interesting implication of my argument, is that it can explain this fact: that is, it can explain why anti-restrictionists do not seem to regard such regulations as examples of *gun control*. If I am right, they aren't.

More interesting is the case of certain other possible regulations, ones that do not already exist nationwide in the United States. I am referring to the possibility of (1) some sort of nationally linked background check for such things as felony convictions prior to purchasing a gun (with no exceptions, such as sales between individuals and sales at gun shows); and (2) some sort of licensing and safety training for purchasing a gun (very roughly similar to the requirements for getting a license to drive a car).[1] Is my argument consistent with these measures?

Purely as a matter of logic, I think the answer is yes. Background checks for relevant criminal convictions (such as violent felonies) are not restrictionist in my sense, since they are not based on the "too many guns out there" premise and since they target a segment of the population that, by its own guilty behavior, has revealed itself to be a violent threat to the rest of us. For some of the same reasons, such a measure is fully compatible with the voluntaristic model. (Background checks to deny guns to felons with no history of violence would presumably be more difficult to justify on such grounds.)

Licensing, with perhaps a safety course requirement, might be argued for on the basis of the principle of risk, and it arguably avoids the fallacy of treating guns per se as on-balance enhancers of risk. The idea behind this sort of measure could be to target not firearms but incompetent or unethical users of firearms. This, too, could be consistent with the voluntaristic model and, indeed, an application of it.

Also compatible with the main line of argument I have offered here would be attempts to discourage suicide by enacting laws that require a before-purchase waiting period or some safe storage requirement such as trigger locks. In that case the idea would be to add a little more time between the initial impulse and the ensuing action, making possible an additional opportunity for reflection.

I do not mean to endorse such supposedly reflection-enabling measures. Aside from doubts as to whether they would work, and would work well enough without offsetting bad effects, there could be other ethical problems with such a regulatory approach.[2] I am merely pointing out the logical limits of the argument I have offered here. An argument based on the Lockean sovereignty-rights I mentioned in chapter 2 would have much more far-reaching implications, but as already discussed, I have not chosen to pursue such a line of reasoning here.

I have said that my argument is not incompatible with such measures purely as a matter of logic. What, you may wonder, could possibly be relevant here, other than logic? I don't think we have to look very far to find the answer to this question. American gun owners and the groups that represent them, such as the National Rifle Association, are opposed the two principal sorts of measures just mentioned—expanded background checks and licensing—in a determined, heels-dug-in manner; and their reasons are related to concerns I have raised here, though the nature of the connection lies in psychology and politics rather than logic alone.

One reason for this recalcitrant attitude is what might be called "the dialogue of the deaf problem." This is the fact that when control activists put forth moderate proposals, partisans for the other side typically are convinced that such measures are merely shrewd tactical moves in a game in which the real purpose is to eventually ban civilian guns, or at least handguns.[3] Indeed, control advocates often unwittingly provide motivation for this attitude by blurting out that one moderate proposal or another would be "a good beginning" or "a first step." (A first step toward what?) They claim that this distrustful attitude on the part of control opponents is simply paranoid because very few people in their movement are advocating or calling for complete prohibition. But what control opponents *hear* in such declarations is that the control activists are not *advocating* or *calling for* firearms bans, and this is not the same thing as disavowing bans as an ultimate strategic goal, or as things that would be favored. It is impossible to have a frank, realistic, and productive dialogue with the opposing side if you cannot not trust their ultimate motives or take their proposals at face value.

There is a related phenomenon that one sometimes sees in the scholarly literature, in which a moderate proposal is backed by arguments that, if they are good arguments, will ultimately justify far stronger measures. This is true of the article by Hugh LaFollette that I have discussed in earlier chapters.[4] The policy proposal he offers falls far short of banning guns, but the philosophical part of his argument consists in showing that there is no serious, weighty right to own a gun at all. If this is an argument for a moderate measure, it is equally well an argument for a complete ban.

Another, more important reason for recalcitrance about moderate regulations—one that reinforces the dialogue of the deaf problem a hundredfold—is what might be called, in a broad sense, "the slippery slope problem." By this I mean various reasons for thinking that a given measure, which may be innocuous or even benign in itself, might make more likely a certain further measure that one regards as noxious.

A more substantive worry is that the first measure might serve as *a mechanism* for bringing about that more noxious one. Joseph Olson and David Kopel argue that this is what happened in England during the twentieth century, when the country was gradually transformed from one in

This, of course, is pure fantasy. We do not live in that America. In our world, people do have veiled agendas and it can it is often very important to know what a person's ultimate goal is. This implies that a policy benign in itself can acquire a different character if there are enough people who have purposes that are not so benign. The English system was friendly to gun owners for years after 1920, until enough people with power and influence decided it should be otherwise. In America today there are already many people who have made the same decision. Unfortunately, this means that a heels-dug-in posture, which seems paranoid to outsiders, is perfectly rational if considered from the anti-restrictionist point of view. Everyone knows that it is rational to evaluate a given policy on the basis of its predicted consequences. Why shouldn't future policies that might result from a given policy be counted as among its consequences? Thus an attitude that looks paranoid from the outside is actually *required* by rationality, if it is judged from inside the individual's point of view. So great is the Great Divide.

The dialogue of the deaf will go on. This is a shame, because it probably is blocking beneficial changes, but at this time I see no practical alternative.

NOTES

1. I say "very roughly" because using a gun safely is a much simpler matter than safely managing a half-ton of metal hurtling through space at 65 mph and controlled by nothing but four points of road-to-tire friction. As someone who is both licensed to drive and has completed a gun safety course, I am

entitled to opine on this subject without citing any authority other than my own experience.

2. On the issue of whether such measures work, see J. Caron, M. Julien, and J. H. Huang, "Changes in Suicide Methods in Quebec between 1987 and 2000: The Possible Impact of Bill C-17 Requiring Safe Storage of Firearms," *Suicide and Life-Threatening Behavior*, 38, no. 2 (April 2008): 195–208. The authors found that although the rate of firearms suicide dropped after passage of a safe-storage law, the rate of suicide by hanging rose and that, moreover, neither trend was statistically significant.

3. I owe the eloquent phrase "dialogue of the deaf" to criminologist Gary Kleck, though I am not sure he means exactly what I mean by it. For his use of the phrase, and numerous quotes in which various pro-control advocates, including President Clinton, speak of one moderate proposal or another as a "first step," see Gary Kleck and Don B. Kates, *Armed: New Perspectives on Gun Control* (Amherst, NY: Prometheus, 2001), 131–38.

4. For his moderate proposal, see Hugh LaFollette, "Gun Control" *Ethics* 110 (January 2000).

5. Joseph E. Olson and David Kopel, "All the Way Down the Slippery Slope: Gun Prohibition in England and Some Lessons for Civil Liberties in America," *Hamline Law Review* 22 (1999): 400. This article is easily available online.

6. Ibid., 423–25.

7. See John R. Lott Jr., *More Guns, Less Crime: Understanding Crime and Gun Control Laws*, 3rd ed. (Chicago: University of Chicago Press, 2010).

PART II

THE CASE IN FAVOR

DAVID DEGRAZIA

their already permissive gun laws. American champions of gun control perceive the influence of the powerful gun lobby, especially the National Rifle Association (NRA), as the primary force behind congressional inaction. By contrast, some gun enthusiasts think the problem with American gun violence is not lax gun regulations but the fact that not enough people are armed. With considerable notoriety, NRA executive vice president Wayne LaPierre proclaimed, shortly after the Newton tragedy, "The only thing that stops a bad guy with a gun is a good guy with a gun."[1]

Although the tragedies in Aurora and Newtown were especially heart-rending, gun massacres and gun violence more generally are frequent occurrences in the United States. In 2012, for example, there were at least fourteen mass shootings.[2] In the same year (the last for which I could obtain reliable data), there were more than 32,000 gun deaths in the United States and more than 81,000 nonfatal gun injuries.[3] American levels of gun violence are extremely high in comparison to rates in other developed countries. Consider data collected by the United Nations on gun homicides in the United States and three other English-speaking, developed nations: Canada, Great Britain (England and Wales), and Australia.[4] In the years 2003 through 2009, the annual rate of gun homicide per 100,000 population averaged about 3.7 in the United States. In our northern next-door neighbor, the rate per 100,000 people averaged just under 0.6. Meanwhile, the average rates in Britain and Australia were 0.1 and just under 0.16, respectively. That means that, in comparison with three countries that have much in common culturally with the United States, the American gun homicide rate, per population size, ranged from just over six times as great to thirty-seven times as great. Also noteworthy is that, among the tens of thousands of Americans killed annually by guns, a great number are children. A major Centers for Disease Control and Prevention (CDC) study found that the firearm death rate among American children was almost twelve times higher than the average rates of twenty-five other developed countries.[5]

Gun violence abounds in the United States as compared with other developed countries. Gun ownership rates are also high by international standards. According to a 2007 study, the United States leads the world with eighty-nine guns per hundred people, with Yemen a distant second at fifty-five guns per hundred people.[6] Although we cannot straightforwardly infer that the high levels of gun violence are causally related to the high gun ownership rates—a point of contention between advocates and opponents of gun control—there is no denying that American rates of gun violence are extremely high compared with other developed countries, and that American gun ownership rates are extremely high compared with other countries more generally.

High ownership rates are presumably related, in part, to gun regulations that make it very easy to purchase and possess firearms in this country. American adults who lack any specific disqualifying criminal or psychiatric history are eligible buyers. While state laws vary, federal exclusionary criteria—such as having a felony conviction or having been committed to a psychiatric institution—leave eligible many people with troubling histories that suggest a degree of dangerousness. Eligible buyers include persons convicted of violent misdemeanors (except domestic violence), individuals with substantial records of alcohol abuse, and many people who have significant psychiatric problems but have not been hospitalized for them; stalkers under temporary restraining orders are not required to surrender firearms they already own. The Brady Handgun Violence Prevention Act mandates background checks of gun buyers, but only if the seller is a licensed dealer. Private sales, including those conducted online or at gun shows, are exempt. (Perhaps surprisingly, there is no age minimum for purchasing long guns from a private seller.) Meanwhile, comprehensive records of background checks are precluded by the Firearm Owners Protection Act, which prohibits creation of a national registry of gun ownership. The same law limited the Bureau of Alcohol, Tobacco, and Firearms (ATF) from inspecting any gun dealer more than once a year and increased the standard of proof needed to revoke licenses. Owing to a 2003 spending bill amendment, law enforcement may not publicly release data showing where criminals bought firearms. As for carrying guns in public, the only federal law is the Gun-Free School Zones Act. Nearly every state permits the carrying of firearms and over thirty require no license to do so. And since the expiration in 2004 of the Federal Assault Weapons Ban Act, guns legally available to the public include not only ordinary handguns and long guns but also "assault weapons"—which (among other features) reload automatically, allowing for more rapid firing—and high-capacity ammunition clips. It is noteworthy that both of the massacres described at the beginning of this chapter, like many others in recent years, featured such weaponry and high-capacity clips.

The foregoing represents a small catalogue of facts about the American gun policy status quo that indicate how permissive it is. One way to put this policy status quo into perspective is to consider how little guns, the products themselves, are regulated. For purposes of comparison, consider automobiles. Car accidents kill many Americans every year—typically a few thousand more than are killed with guns. Unlike guns, cars are used on an everyday basis and are not designed to be dangerous, but a moving car can cause a great deal of harm.[7] Between 1920 and 1960, American automobile policy was dominated by the auto-mobile industry, which tried to blame car accidents on irresponsible drivers. But scientific research on car crashes led to more of a public health approach—that is, looking to prevent accidents rather than to blame someone after they occur—beginning in the 1960s. This shift led to such safety features as seat belts, better brakes, padded dash-boards, shatter-resistant windshields, and airbags. Many such safety features have been mandated by federal or state laws, and the percentage of automobile fatalities per mile driven has plummeted since the 1950s. American society, quite sensibly, regulates car design to promote safety. In fact, it regulates nearly all consumer products, including medicines, medicine bottles, particular foods, vitamins, clothes, and children's toys. Yet guns, which are about the most dangerous product a person can legally buy, are almost entirely unregulated—not even for purposes of child-proofing. And, as with the product, so with the manufacturer: The 2005 Protection of Lawful Commerce in Arms Act granted the gun industry immunity from legal liability.

Thus, the American gun status quo is characterized by high levels of gun violence and ownership, as well as minimal gun regulations. Let us complete this sketch of the status quo by briefly considering American attitudes toward guns. In sum, Americans tend to believe *both* in gun rights and in gun control. Strong majorities of Americans polled support the proposition that competent, law-abiding adults should be permitted to purchase at least some types of firearms such as ordinary handguns and long guns.[8] At the same time, polls consistently show that a majority (or at least a plurality) state that gun control laws should be made stricter rather than less strict or kept the same; moreover, the numerical gulf between those favoring strict gun control and those who oppose it is substantial.[9] As we will see in chapter 10, American attitudes are consistent with the most recent gun-related rulings of the U.S. Supreme Court.

DISTINGUISHING SEVERAL ISSUES

This book addresses the issue of what extent of gun control is morally defensible. Thus, the book addresses *ethics at the level of public policy*, gun policy in particular. But the ethics of gun control, or of gun policy, is connected with the ethics of owning and carrying guns, which concerns decisions by individuals. Let us now distinguish, more explicitly, several issues within the gambit of what we might broadly term "gun ethics" and clarify which issues will be addressed here.

A comprehensive view of gun ethics would address the following questions. First, do private citizens (as opposed to police officers and military personnel) have a moral right to own guns and, more specifically, an "undefeated" moral right (which is to say, a moral right that is not overridden by competing moral rights or by appeal to the general welfare)? If so, do private citizens have an undefeated moral right to carry their guns in public and/or to hunt animals with their weapons? (The concept of a moral right will be elucidated in chapter 10.) Finally, what is the appropriate shape of government controls on private gun ownership?

My discussion will focus on the last question. Thus, it focuses on what gun policies are morally defensible—with particular attention to American policy. Relatedly, it gives sustained attention to the issue of whether individuals have a moral right to gun ownership. Space constraints will preclude addressing the ethics of carrying firearms and the ethics of hunting, except for a few remarks in passing.

With its emphasis on ethics, my discussion is *not* primarily a legal analysis. Nevertheless, just as the discussion in the previous section of this chapter included references to current law, the ethical analysis of gun policy will have to take current policy, including laws, into account while presenting a view of which policies, including laws, would be ethically justifiable.

TYPES OF GUNS AND THE CONCEPT OF GUN CONTROL

In discussing the ethics of gun control, it will help to have at least a rough understanding of what sorts of guns there are and what the term "gun control" will mean in the discussion.

Although guns may be characterized and classified in any number of ways, I find it helpful to distinguish types of guns—or firearms—by reference to (1) their basic

configuration and (2) how they load and fire. As for configuration, guns are usually divided into *handguns*, which are
relatively small and easily held in one hand, and *long guns*,
which include rifles and shotguns. Today, at least in the
United States, handguns are owned primarily for purposes
of self-defense while long guns are owned primarily for
hunting or target shooting. Handguns are also used more
often than long guns in criminal activities, which is why
some gun control proponents favor banning handguns but
not necessarily long guns.

Among those who oppose banning handguns, much
less all guns, the second way of classifying guns, according to how they load and fire, may seem more relevant to
discussions of gun control. The distinctions here concern
"automaticity"—how automatic a gun is—and the three
important categories are *manual, semi-automatic*, and *automatic*. (Note that these three categories cut across the
distinction between handguns and long guns.) Manual
firearms must be loaded for each shot, and each shot
requires a separate pull of the trigger. Semi-automatic firearms do not need to be reloaded after each shot, allowing
them to be fired more quickly than manual guns, but each
shot requires a trigger pull. By contrast, automatic firearms, such as machine guns and submachine guns, fire the
fastest because they do not require reloading for each shot
and they continue firing for as long as the shooter holds
down the trigger. Whereas automatic firearms are highly
regulated and difficult to obtain,[10] semi-automatic guns
are largely unregulated and readily available.

My classification has not mentioned assault weapons.
That is because the very term "assault weapon" represents
a point of dispute in the debate over gun control. Gun

control proponents are more likely to use the term in order to designate a class of firearms they believe to be unnecessarily dangerous for legitimate purposes. Of course, the 1994 Assault Weapons Ban (which was allowed to lapse in 2004) used the term, but offered a complex set of criteria for what sorts of weapons would count as assault weapons; and the law was subject to many loopholes, failing to cover all firearms within the original spirit of the legislation. I will use the term "assault weapon" sparingly. I suggest that we understand it, roughly, as designating semi-automatic firearms that have detachable ammunition clips and are designed for rapid firing, especially if the firearms possess certain other military-style features such as a pistol grip and a folding or telescoping stock. These weapons have been used—sometimes with chilling effectiveness—in many of the massacres that have occurred in the United States in recent decades.[11]

And what does "gun control" refer to? I understand this term to designate laws and policies designed to restrict the manufacture, sale, possession, storage, transfer, or use of firearms and/or associated ammunition in the interest of public safety. Examples include laws that prohibit the manufacture of machine guns, laws that prevent felons or psychiatrically ill persons from purchasing guns, and laws that require licensed sellers to conduct background checks on prospective buyers. In discussing gun control, however, I will consider not only gun control measures as just defined but also related political measures. These include policies that permit government agencies to study the causes of gun violence and the effectiveness or ineffectiveness of various gun regulations, as well as policies that strengthen the ATF's ability to study where guns used in crimes were originally sold and the paths they took in reaching criminal hands.

PLAN FOR REMAINING CHAPTERS

In the remaining chapters, I will defend gun control that is considerably more extensive than currently exists in the United States. We might describe my position as defending *moderately extensive* or *relatively extensive* gun control. Rather than continually using these cumbersome qualifiers, I will usually just speak of "gun control." The linguistic shortcut will be harmless as long as readers remember that no sane person—and certainly not my coauthor, Lester Hunt—advocates a complete absence of gun regulations. No sane person, for example, thinks that our society ought to make machine guns available to young children. So the real issue debated in this book is not whether *any* gun control is justified, but whether relatively extensive or relatively little gun control is justified.

Chapter 10, "Law, Ethics, and Responsible Public Policy," opens with a brief discussion of the Second Amendment to the Constitution, which, according to recent decisions by the U.S. Supreme Court, confers a legal right to private firearm ownership. After presenting reasons to doubt the court's reading of the Second Amendment, I will emphasize that, as the Supreme Court explicitly recognized, asserting a constitutional right to bear arms is consistent with significant restrictions on the design, ownership, and use of guns. I will also underscore my discussion's emphasis on ethics, rather than law, as well as its focus on public policy.

Finally, I will clarify the concept of moral rights, a concept central to the debate over gun control.

The next two chapters reconstruct and criticize major arguments against gun control. Chapter 11, "Critique of Appeals to Self-Defense and Physical Security," challenges several assumptions in the reasoning that underlies such appeals, which attempt to establish an undefeated right to private gun ownership and, on the basis of such a right, a case against gun control. Although I cast doubt on the existence of such a right, it becomes apparent that the case for a right is much stronger than the case against gun control. In chapter 12, "Critique of Appeals to Liberty Rights," I reconstruct and argue against (1) the assertion of a fundamental right to own guns, (2) the appeal to freedom to pursue one's own conception of the good life as a basis for gun rights, and (3) the appeal to freedom from tyranny as an argument against gun control.

The next two chapters present a positive case for gun control. Chapter 13, "The Consequentialist Case for Gun Control," appeals to the social consequences of gun ownership, especially where minimal regulation prevails, and argues that much stronger gun regulations are needed in the interest of public safety. Along the way, I argue that the case for banning private gun ownership is much stronger than is generally realized. Nevertheless, the case for a ban is much more difficult to make than the case for gun control, so I do not defend the more questionable thesis. Chapter 14, "The Rights-Based Case for Gun Control," responds to the claim that a moral right to gun ownership exists independently of social consequences, whether positive or negative on balance, and militates against gun control. My reply turns this emphasis on rights on its head by emphasizing the need to *enforce* rights that would be violated if one were shot—as is more likely where gun regulations are lax. I also defend a right to a reasonably safe environment and demonstrate that reconciling this right with a right to bear arms requires gun control.

Chapter 15, "Gun Politics in the United States," presents examples to illustrate the extreme state of American gun policy and gun culture, before attempting to explain how such an extreme status quo is possible. The discussion emphasizes the distinction between political feasibility and ethical defensibility, paving the way for chapter 16, "Policy Recommendations." In this final chapter, I briefly outline gun control regulations—beyond those currently in place—that I recommend in view of the arguments developed in my part of the book.

NOTES

1. David Nakamura and Tom Hamburger, "Put Armed Police in Every School, NRA Urges," *Washington Post*, December 21, 2012, 1.
2. See Bonnie Berkowitz and Alberto Cuadra, "U.S. Mass Shootings in 2012," *Washington Post*, December 15, 2012, A14; and George Walsh, "Man Who Set Trap for Firefighters Left Note About Plan," *Washington Post*, December 26, 2012, A3.
3. Centers for Disease Control and Prevention, Web-based Injury Statistics Query and Reporting System, www.cdc.gov/injury/wisqars/index.html; accessed March 27, 2015.
4. United Nations Office on Drugs and Crime, "International Rates of Gun Homicides," www.unodc.org; 2011 Excel document accessed January 2, 2014.

5. Centers for Disease Control and Prevention, "Rates of Homicide, Suicide, and Firearm-related Death among Children—26 Industrialized Countries," *Morbidity and Mortality Weekly Report* 46 (February 7, 1997): 101–105.

6. Geneva Graduate Institute of International Studies, *Small Arms Survey 2007* (Cambridge: Cambridge University Press, 2007).

7. The remainder of this paragraph is indebted to David Hemenway, *Private Guns, Public Health* (Ann Arbor: University of Michigan Press, 2010), 12–17.

8. See, e.g., CNN/Opinion Research Corporation polls conducted June 2008 and May 2009; Pew Research Center poll conducted March 2010; and ABC News/Washington Post poll conducted January 2011 (results of all four polls presented in PollingReport.com at www.pollingreport.com/guns.htm).

9. See, e.g., Gallup Poll conducted October 2010, CBS News/New York Times poll conducted January 2011, Time Poll conducted June 2011, NBC/Wall Street Journal Poll conducted January 2011, ABC News/Washington Post Poll conducted January 2011, and CBS News Poll conducted January 2011 (results presented in PollingReport.com at www.pollingreport.com/guns.htm); Robert Spitzer, *The Politics of Gun Control*, 5th ed. (Boulder, CO: Paradigm, 2012), 119; and Emma McGinty, Daniel Webster, Jon Vernick, and Colleen Barry, "Public Opinion on Proposals to Strengthen U.S. Gun Laws," in Daniel Webster and Jon Vernick, eds., *Reducing Gun Violence in America* (Baltimore: Johns Hopkins University Press, 2013), 239–57.

10. The National Firearms Act (1934), Gun Control Act (1968), and the 1968 Hughes Amendment placed strict limits on how automatic weapons can be obtained and sold. Obtaining such a weapon requires an extensive FBI background check and a substantial tax, and only those made and registered with the federal government before 1986 can be owned or sold.

11. Alberto Cuadra et al., "Weapons and Mass Shootings," *Washington Post*, June 1, 2014, A14.

10

Law, Ethics, and Responsible Public Policy

■□■

THIS IS A BOOK ABOUT the ethics of gun control. It addresses law from the standpoint of ethics: what gun policies we *ought (morally) to have*. In doing so, however, it must take into account the legal status quo. One part of the status quo, and a touchstone of current public discussions of gun rights and gun control, is the Second Amendment to the U.S. Constitution. After discussing the Second Amendment at some length, this chapter will consider the role of ethics in the debate over guns. It will then examine the concept of moral rights and consider what it means to assert a moral right to private gun ownership.

THE SECOND AMENDMENT

The Second Amendment reads as follows: "A well regulated Militia, being necessary to the security of a free State, the right of the people to keep and bear Arms, shall not be infringed." What exactly does this mean? What is the significance of the reference to a militia? Should the Second

Amendment be interpreted to assert a *private* right to bear arms—that is, a right of private citizens to own guns *even if not serving in militias*?

On the most natural reading of this sentence, the reference to a militia is significant. Otherwise, why make the reference? The centrality of militias is even more explicit in draft language for the amendment submitted by James Madison (even if the clause following the semicolon addresses a separate concern): "A well-regulated militia, composed of the body of the people, being the best security of a free state, the right of the people to keep and bear arms shall not be infringed; but no person religiously scrupulous shall be compelled to bear arms."[1]

Militias were an important part of American life at the time the Constitution was written. They were valued for (1) their availability to resist foreign invasion and attack by Native Americans, (2) their ability to squash insurrection by individuals within a state, and (3) the protection they offered if the new federal government abused its power and threatened the state's people in some way. At the time, a substantial national military presence, or standing army, had yet to be established. Anti-federalists wanted a constitutional guarantee that the federal government could not disarm state militias. So, above all, the amendment—on the most natural reading in historical context—concerned the relationship between the states and the new federal government, and it represented a compromise between federalists and anti-federalists: a federal government, yes, but only if states may retain armed militias.[2] Consequently, the Second Amendment does not address, much less assert, a right to bear arms independently of military service.

For many years, the U.S. Supreme Court agreed with this reading. As former Supreme Court Justice John Paul Stevens explains, for more than two centuries after adoption of the amendment, federal judges agreed that the right protected by the text applied only to bearing arms for military purposes and imposed no limits on the power of states or local governments to regulate ownership or use of firearms.[3] Stevens points to the example of *United States v. Miller* (1939), in which a unanimous court held that Congress could prohibit possession of sawed-off shotguns *because such a weapon had no reasonable relation to the work of "a well regulated Militia."*

It was not until deciding *District of Columbia v. Heller* in 2008 that the Supreme Court interpreted the Second Amendment as guaranteeing a private right to bear arms.[4] At issue were Washington, D.C.'s handgun ban and its requirement to keep firearms dissembled or bound by a trigger lock. Writing for the bare 5–4 majority, Justice Antonin Scalia asserted that both provisions of the D.C. law were unconstitutional and, more generally, that the Second Amendment guarantees an individual's right to possess a firearm (independently of militia service) and to use that firearm for such lawful purposes as self-defense in the home. Technically, the *Heller* decision was limited to federal enclaves such as Washington, D.C. Two years later the court's reasoning was extended in *McDonald v. City of Chicago*, which affirmed that the right to own guns applied to the states.[5]

While encouraged and subsequently lauded by the gun lobby, the majority's fresh interpretation of the Second Amendment was subject to pointed critique, beginning with the four dissenting justices in each of two statements. Justice Stevens interpreted the amendment as protecting states' interest in safeguarding their sovereignty against the new federal government, which was empowered to create a standing army. He argued that the majority produced no historical evidence that the Constitution's Framers wanted to limit legislatures' authority to regulate or ban civilian use of weapons.[6] In the other dissent, Justice Stephen Breyer similarly argued that the Second Amendment protects militia-related interests rather than interests in private self-defense. More distinctively, he contended that even if there is a constitutional right to private gun ownership, the sorts of regulations imposed by Washington, D.C. might be permissible in crime-ridden urban areas. Breyer proposed that firearm laws be evaluated by balancing the interests protected by the right to gun ownership against the state's interests in public safety and fighting crime, an approach that would permit the right to be overridden in some circumstances.[7]

Scholars from both the left and the right of the political spectrum have criticized the majority's reasoning. For example, liberal political science professor Robert Spitzer writes: "The *Heller* and *McDonald* rulings have established as a matter of law an individual rights interpretation of the Second Amendment. But although judges can change the law, they cannot change history, and the historical record largely contradicts the bases for these two recent rulings."[8] Richard Posner, a prominent conservative legal scholar, has argued that "professional historians were on [Justice] Stephens' side" and that the majority ruling provides "evidence of the ability of well-staffed courts to produce snow jobs."[9] These critiques are consistent with what I characterize as a natural reading of the Second Amendment in historical context.

While the Supreme Court's recent decisions are noted primarily for supporting a constitutional right to bear arms, it is equally important that these rulings are circumspect about the breadth of this right—how much it covers—while explicitly asserting the constitutionality of gun control. Although the National Rifle Association (NRA) encourages its members to believe that gun control measures are a threat to or violation of the right to bear arms, the Supreme Court disagrees:

> Like most rights, the Second Amendment right is not unlimited. It is not a right to keep and carry any weapon whatsoever in any manner whatsoever and for whatever purpose. For example, concealed weapons prohibitions have been upheld under the Amendment or state analogues. The Court's opinion should not be taken to cast doubt on longstanding prohibitions on the possession of firearms by felons and the mentally ill, or laws forbidding the carrying of firearms in sensitive places such as schools and government buildings, or laws imposing conditions and qualifications on the commercial sale of arms. *Miller*'s holding that the sorts of weapons protected are those "in common use at the time" finds support in the historical tradition of prohibiting the carrying of dangerous and unusual weapons.[10]

So the same Supreme Court that asserts a right to bear arms asserts that this right may be subject to significant limitations. In fact, the court suggests several limits on gun rights that would pass constitutional muster. The last sentence, for example, opens legal space for a ban on semi-automatic weapons with high-capacity clips. It also deserves emphasis that, in asserting a constitutional right to bear arms, the court left open whether there is a right to carry guns in public.

THE ROLE OF ETHICS

According to the legal interpretation that prevails today, Americans have a right to private gun ownership—which I will usually refer to as a "right to gun ownership" or "right to bear arms," for short. In this sense, there is a legal right to bear arms in the United States. Yet, as mentioned in chapter 9, this fact leaves considerable space for ethical discussion of gun policy.

For one thing, the Supreme Court's rulings are not immune to challenge. It is quite conceivable that at some future time the court, with different membership, will reverse the decisions of *Heller* and *McDonald* and decide that there is no right to bear arms independently of military service—or that, if there is such a right, it may in some circumstances be overridden by concerns about public safety and law enforcement (as Justice Breyer suggested). Alternatively, these decisions could be overruled by a new amendment to the Constitution or a new congressional statute. As an example of such congressional trumping of the Supreme Court, the Supreme Court's decision in *Dred Scott v. Sanford* (60 U.S. 393 [1857]), to the effect that African Americans could not be American citizens, was overturned by both the Civil Rights Act of 1866 and, after some members of Congress challenged the Act's authority, the Fourteenth Amendment, which passed in 1868. So the legal judgment that there is a right to bear arms is not set in stone. Consequently, there is room to debate what

American law regarding this putative right *should be*. In my opinion—with which, I recognize, many legal scholars and philosophers of law would disagree—the most appropriate approach to addressing this question would include considerations of ethics.

Even if we took a legal right to bear arms as (legally) set in stone, we would need to consider what sorts of gun policies are socially responsible within this legal regime. Ethical analysis has much to contribute to this discussion. What gun control measures are legitimate is a question the court left fairly open and one that invites the input of ethical reasoning.

In addition, it is an important matter whether the legal right to bear arms is undergirded by a *moral* right to bear arms, as many gun advocates believe. If the legal right is supported in this way, then it enjoys an especially powerful backing: not only the Constitution but also a moral right that is independent of the Constitution. Perhaps, assuming again for discussion's sake that the Constitution guarantees a right to gun ownership, the Framers had the prior moral right in mind in writing the Second Amendment as they did. No doubt some gun enthusiasts think so. If this view is correct (as I doubt), then overturning the Supreme Court's recent gun rights rulings in the future would constitute a sort of legal violence against a moral right to bear arms. Or, to put the idea hypothetically, had the Supreme Court decided in recent cases that there is *not* a Constitutional right to gun ownership, gun advocates who believe in a moral right to bear arms would probably believe that, whatever the Constitution might say (or be interpreted to say), current laws *should* permit private gun ownership.

These reflections help to explain why an ethical investigation of gun rights and gun control is worthwhile. Because much of the focus will be on the assertion of a moral right to gun ownership, we will consider what moral rights are and what a moral right to gun ownership would amount to.

MORAL RIGHTS

There are various kinds of rights. These include *legal* rights, as just discussed, and *institutional* rights such as the right of a faculty member in the George Washington University Department of Philosophy to review a report on her teaching before it is submitted to the Department Chair. There is, additionally, the discourse of *human* rights—roughly, rights one has simply in virtue of being a human being or person—a plausible example of which is a right against enslavement. But perhaps we have some *moral* rights not because we are human beings or persons, but because of particular circumstances such as having entered into an agreement (e.g., my right against you that you keep your solemn promise to me) or being a member of a prosperous society (e.g., a right to a measure of financial security in old age).[11] I understand moral rights to represent a broader category than human rights (even if human rights can also be legal and/or political-institutional rights). And it is more important whether there is a moral right to gun ownership than whether such a right is also a human right. After all, it seems possible that members of some societies, partly in view of their circumstances and state of technology, have a right to gun ownership whereas members of some other societies do not.[12]

So what is a moral right? It is a right that is *grounded in the requirements of morality*. And what are rights, more generally? Rights have been analyzed as involving one or more of four elements—privileges (liberties), claims, powers, and immunities—but I will follow the originator of this classification in holding that only claims are rights "in the strictest sense."[13] Thus, I concentrate on what are sometimes called *claim rights*.

According to John Stuart Mill, "[w]hen we call anything a person's right, we mean that he has a valid claim on society to protect him in the possession of it."[14] Somewhat similarly, Henry Shue asserts of moral rights in particular that such a right "provides (1) the rational basis for a justified demand (2) that the actual enjoyment of a substance [the object of the right] be (3) socially guaranteed against standard threats."[15] Mill and Shue plausibly assert that moral rights, or at least many of them, have an importance that justifies an expectation that society will protect one's possession of the thing (e.g., freedom of speech) to which one has a right. But this may not be true of all rights. For example, I may have a moral right against you to your keeping your promise to me, but society need not involve itself in this matter. Feinberg understands rights simply as valid claims,[16] a conception that does not necessarily implicate society as protector of the right. But more specificity would be helpful.

Providing such specificity while maintaining plausibility, Raz proposes that one has a right only if an aspect of one's well-being—that is, an interest one has—provides a sufficient reason to hold someone else to be under a duty.[17] I believe this is on the right conceptual track.[18] Moral rights, I further assume (in agreement with most gun advocates[19]), generally resist appeals to utility as grounds to override the rights. They are strict, even if not absolute, moral protections.[20] In sum, *moral rights are valid moral claims that protect important interests and ordinarily trump appeals to the general welfare.* I leave open whether, in addition, such claims qualify as moral rights only if they place society under an obligation to provide reasonable protection of the interests in question against standard threats.

Several distinctions among kinds of moral rights will be important in considering gun rights. One is the classic distinction between so-called *negative* and *positive* rights. The former are conceptualized as rights of noninterference, the latter as rights to be provided with something. For example, one might hold that you have a negative right to free speech, requiring others to allow you to speak freely, and a positive right to basic education, which society is required to provide you. Theorists who stress this distinction tend to believe that the existence of negative rights is less disputable than the existence of positive rights, that negative rights are easier to fulfill than positive rights, and that the former take moral priority over the latter if the two ever conflict.

Increasingly, the conceptual and moral priority traditionally accorded to negative rights is questioned along with the clarity and usefulness of the distinction itself.[21] To cite one reason for these doubts, meaningful exercise of important negative rights requires substantial positive steps from society to protect the rights-bearers from standard threats. For example, the negative right to free speech has little value if one isn't protected from assault by those who dislike what one has to say and if courts do not punish those who commit assaults. But, of course, effective police and reliable courts, not to mention prisons, represent a substantial public investment. Also, it is sometimes harder or more costly to respect negative rights than to respect positive rights. For example, the cost of respecting a drug company's (negative) property right in a patent for a life-saving medication, by letting the company set prices as high as it wishes, may be the loss of millions of human lives, whereas the cost of respecting those people's right to life-saving medication may be nothing more than a lower profit margin.

Although much traditional thinking about negative and positive rights is dubious, a rough distinction between the two kinds of rights may sometimes be helpful. Presumably, for example, the putative moral right to gun ownership would be a negative right, a right not to be prevented by society from owning guns. It would not, at least as gun advocates understand it, constitute an entitlement to be provided by society with guns.

Also important to our discussion are limits to rights, of which there are two primary kinds. First, there are limits to the *scope* of any particular right. For example, your right to freedom of bodily movement permits you to do many things: exercise in your house, stroll through the city, and dance in the park. But it does not include a prerogative to walk into someone else's house without permission or to hit someone in the face. These limits, importantly, are limits of scope. Your right to free movement does not extend as far as entering other people's property or touching their bodies without permission. It's not as if your right includes such actions but is overridden by other people's rights to property and bodily integrity. There is no conflict of rights in such cases because your right to free movement only extends so far; it is limited by other people's rights to bodily integrity and property. If a friend invites you into his house, or invites you to try to hit him in a boxing match, your doing so is permissible, but not in virtue of a right to free movement; rather, it is a permission (not a claim-right) conferred by someone's voluntary agreement.

In addition to being limited in scope, moral rights can be *overridden*. The scope of your right to free movement includes the right to walk around the streets in the city. But, if police arrive on a crime scene and (appropriately) order everyone to remain on the premises for the time being, your right to walk around the city streets is temporarily overridden by society's interest in facilitating police efforts to apprehend felons.

If there is a moral right to gun ownership, it will have limits. For example, it might apply to ordinary long guns and handguns but not semi-automatic weapons. The scope of weapons that the right encompasses might be limited by the legitimate purposes of gun ownership and the uses to which particular types of guns are ordinarily put. Also limited will be the scope of its possessors: children, the seriously mentally ill, felons, and others will be excluded as unfit to possess firearms. Moreover, even among those who possess the right, and within its limited scope, there may be situations in which it is justifiably overridden. To cite an extreme hypothetical, suppose that in recent years 50 percent of all schoolchildren whose families owned firearms killed themselves or someone else with these weapons—despite requirements for safety locks and other appropriate safety measures. In this scenario, the right to own guns might be overridden by forbidding the purchase of new guns or confiscating those already owned until reasonable safety is restored to households in the community. That rights may *sometimes* be justifiably overridden is consistent with the point that they *ordinarily* trump appeals to the general welfare. The hypothetical circumstances just sketched are far from ordinary.

A final distinction that bears on our discussion is that between *basic* rights and *derivative* rights. A basic right, as I will use the term, is a moral right whose fulfillment (1) protects highly general interests that are vital to the prospects for having a reasonably healthy, active life of normal length, and (2) is needed for one's enjoyment of rights generally.[22] Plausible examples of basic rights are rights to physical security and to freedom of movement. A derived right, by contrast, is a right that is more specific than a basic right and is derivable from one or more basic rights. For example, a right not to be assaulted is more specific than, and derivable from, a basic right to physical security. Sometimes particular societal circumstances will determine whether one has a derived right. For example, one's right not to be shot (assuming one is not threatening a massive violation of someone else's rights) can be derived from the right not to be assaulted and, ultimately, the right to physical security, but its existence is contingent upon the existence of firearms.

Importantly, a moral right to gun ownership would not be basic. It is not the case that owning guns, in and of itself, is necessary for the prospect of a decent human life. For one thing, many people who have decent lives do not have guns (or family members who do). Nor is gun ownership necessary for the protection of one's enjoyment of rights generally. My enjoyment of rights to freedom of expression, freedom of movement, and a decent basic education have never required me to have a gun. This suggests that gun rights, if they exist, must be derivative from basic rights in particular societal circumstances.

To sum up: *A right to private gun ownership, if it exists, is a negative, nonabsolute, derivative moral right whose existence in a particular society at a particular time depends on its role in enabling the realization of one or more basic rights.* With this conceptual background, we are well positioned to proceed to the ethics of gun ownership and gun policy.

NOTES

1. Quoted in David Hemenway, *Private Guns, Public Health* (Ann Arbor: University of Michigan Press, 2010), 155.
2. For good discussions of the historical context, see Hemenway, *Private Guns*, 152–56; and Robert Spitzer, *The Politics of Gun Control*, 5th ed. (Boulder, CO: Paradigm, 2012), 21–29.
3. John Paul Stevens, "A Second Opinion on the Second Amendment," *Washington Post*, April 11, 2014, B1, B4. See also Spitzer, *The Politics of Gun Control*, 32–35.
4. *District of Columbia v. Heller*, 554 U.S. 570 (2008).
5. *McDonald v. City of Chicago*, 561 U.S. 3025 (2010).
6. *District of Columbia v. Heller*, 554 U.S. 570 (2008), Justice Stevens (dissenting).
7. *District of Columbia v. Heller*, 554 U.S. 570 (2008), Justice Breyer (dissenting).
8. Spitzer, *The Politics of Gun Control*, 39.
9. "In Defense of Looseness," *The New Republic*, August 27, 2008, http://www.newrepublic.com/article/books/defense-looseness.

10. *District of Columbia v. Heller*, 128 S.Ct. 2783 (2008) (syllabus). The passage makes reference to *United States v. Miller*, 307 U.S. 174 (1939).

11. Also, at least some of our moral rights may be based on traits we share with some nonhuman animals. Perhaps, for example, a right not to be subjected to cruelty is based on sentience, the basic capacity to have feelings, not on anything specific to human beings or persons.

12. For example, ancient Egyptians arguably had a right to bear weapons they could use in self-defense, but it would be silly to say that they had a right to own guns.

13. Wesley Hohfeld, "Some Fundamental Legal Conceptions as Applied in Judicial Reasoning," *Yale Law Journal* 23 (1913): 28–59.

14. John Stuart Mill, *Utilitarianism* (1863), ch. V.

15. Henry Shue, *Basic Rights*, 2nd ed. (Princeton: Princeton University Press, 1996), 13.

16. Joel Feinberg, "On the Nature and Value of Rights," *Journal of Value Inquiry* 4 (1970): 243–57.

17. Joseph Raz, "On the Nature of Rights," *Mind* 93 (1984): 194–214.

18. Thus, in the scholarly debate over the function of rights, I believe that the *interest theory*—which holds that the function of rights is to protect important interests—is closer to the mark than the *will theory*, which holds that the function of rights is to give its holders control over other people's duties (for the will theory, see, e.g., H. L. A. Hart, *Essays on Bentham* [Oxford: Clarendon, 1982]; and Carl Wellman, *Real Rights* [New York: Oxford University Press, 1995]). One reason I reject the will theory is that it implies young children and infants have no moral rights. For excellent recent contributions to this debate, see Gopal Sreenivasan, "A Hybrid Theory of Claim-Rights," *Oxford Journal of Legal Studies* 25 (2005): 257–74; and Leif Wenar, "The Nature of Claim-Rights," *Ethics* 123 (2013): 202–29.

19. See, e.g., Michael Huemer, "Is There a Right to Own a Gun?" *Social Theory and Practice* 29 (2003): 297–324; and

Samuel Wheeler, "Self-Defense: Rights and Coerced Risk-Acceptance," *Public Affairs Quarterly* 11 (1997): 431–43.

20. In contending that rights present strict moral protections that generally resist appeals to utility, I agree with Robert Nozick (*Anarchy, State, and Utopia* [New York: Basic Books, 1974]) and Ronald Dworkin, *Taking Rights Seriously* [London: Duckworth, 1977]. At the same time, I believe that their theories attribute excessive strictness to rights and underestimate the importance of positive rights.

21. See Jeremy Waldron, *Liberal Rights* (Cambridge: Cambridge University Press, 1993), and Shue, *Basic Rights*. Both authors argue that the important distinction is not among rights—negative versus positive—but, rather, among the duties that correlate to rights. Shue argues that all basic or fundamental rights (and most moral rights more generally) correlate to (1) duties to avoid depriving, (2) duties to protect from deprivation, and (3) duties to aid the deprived (*Basic Rights,* 51–55). Somewhat similarly, Waldron asserts that each right correlates to "successive waves of duty, some of them duties of omission, some of them duties of commission, some of them too complicated to fit easily under either heading" (*Liberal Rights*, 25).

22. This bears the influence of Shue's analysis (*Basic Rights*, 18).

11

Critique of Appeals to Self-Defense and Physical Security

■□■

ARGUMENTS IN FAVOR OF GUN rights and against gun control come in a variety of flavors. In the United States, many of these arguments appeal to the Second Amendment to the Constitution. But, as discussed in chapter 10, the Second Amendment is highly ambiguous regarding a right to private gun ownership and, as the Supreme Court recognized, does not preclude significant gun regulations in any case. More important, the present discussion focuses on ethics, not law, with the goal of illuminating morally responsible public policy. Furthermore, thoughtful gun advocates believe that a moral right to gun ownership underlies the legal right that the Supreme Court recently asserted; had the legal right been denied, gun advocates would have claimed that their gun rights had been improperly denied. That, again, is why we will consider leading arguments for a *moral* right to gun ownership.

In this chapter, we will focus on what may be the strongest argument for a moral right to gun ownership. Like the

Supreme Court's analysis of the Second Amendment, which identified self-defense in the home as a legitimate purpose for gun ownership, the argument I will reconstruct appeals to self-defense. And insofar as I will focus on gun *ownership* rather than the carrying of guns in public, I, too, will emphasize self-defense *in the home*. At the same time, rather than simply taking a right to self-defense as axiomatic, I will examine its most plausible basis: *physical security*. Because gun owners have an interest in defending not only themselves but also family members and others who may be present in the household, I will interpret references to "self-defense" broadly to include anyone in the home whom a gun owner may wish to protect. Although this expanded reference of "*self*-defense" exceeds the term's usual meaning, it is clearly within the spirit of what gun advocates have in mind in appealing to self-defense in the home as a basis for gun rights.

THE ARGUMENT FROM PHYSICAL SECURITY

I set out the Argument from Physical Security[1]— contextualized to the American situation—in numbered statements to facilitate easy reference to particular steps. Consistent with the terminology introduced in chapter 10, *basic* rights will be understood as a type of moral right.

1. People have a basic right to physical security.
2. This right is violated by (unjustified) assaults and is threatened by burglaries.

3. People have a moral right to take necessary measures to prevent their basic rights from being violated.

4. The right to take such measures supports a moral right to self-defense.

5. The right to self-defense includes the freedom to use adequate means to defend oneself.

6. In present-day circumstances in the United States, adequate self-defense requires that competent adults have the option of gun ownership.

7. Thus, competent adults in the United States today have a moral right to gun ownership.

8. This right is not justifiably overridden by appeal to the general welfare or by any conflicting moral right—at least in the case of competent, law-abiding adults.

9. So competent, law-abiding adults' moral right to gun ownership should be protected by law in the United States today.

The Argument from Physical Security is an argument for a moral right to gun ownership that is not overridden by competing considerations and therefore demands protection by the American legal system. It's an argument *for gun rights*. But, with an additional step, it can become an argument *against gun control* of the sort I defend:

10. Appropriate legal protection of the moral right to gun ownership in the United States today is incompatible with moderately extensive gun control.

EXAMINATION OF THE FIRST HALF OF THE ARGUMENT—AND REFORMULATION

Having presented the Argument from Physical Security (*APS*, for short), let us flesh out some of the underlying thinking and evaluate its cogency. Critical analysis of the first half of APS will motivate a reformulation in the interest of strengthening the argument.

Step 1 asserts a basic right to physical security. Although the extent of this right is controversial, the idea that people have some sort of basic right to physical security is extremely plausible. This basic right may be understood as underlying other rights that we tend to believe people have, including rights not to be assaulted, killed, tortured, and raped. I concur that there is a basic right to physical security, while recognizing that its extent—for example, does it include a right to access to health care?—is uncertain and debatable.

Step 2 claims that the right to physical security is violated by unjustified assaults and threatened by burglaries. The reason for specifying *unjustified* assaults is the plausible idea that one's right to physical security is not violated if one is *justifiably* assaulted—for example, when a police officer uses necessary force to prevent someone from seriously harming another person. But unjustified assaults violate one's right to physical security. Moreover, burglaries threaten this right insofar as someone breaking into your home may very well assault you. Burglars also pose a threat to your property. I assume that people have rights over disposition of their property even if (as I suspect) these rights are not basic ones. So far, then, I fully agree with APS.

Step 3 asserts that people have a moral right to take necessary measures to prevent violation of their basic rights. Although this may seem obvious, it is here that I entertain my first doubts. Suppose I know that an assassin is trying to kill me (an innocent person), an action that would violate my rights. Presumably, I have a right to try to prevent this from happening. But what if the only way I could prevent this from happening were by blowing up a large portion of the crowded building in which he is staying, killing not only him but also dozens of innocent people? I have no right to do so, even if doing so is necessary to prevent the assassin from killing me. My act of self-defense in this case would be disproportionately harmful to innocent others and would violate their rights. My right to self-defense is qualified by limits to the means I may take.

Let us preserve what seems right about step 3, while correcting what seems wrong, by reformulating it as follows: 3. *People have a moral right to take necessary measures to prevent their basic rights from being violated—so long as these measures do not involve illegitimately harming or violating the rights of others.* With this more guarded formulation of the argument's third step, a proponent of APS is likely to be confident about step 4: The latter right supports a moral right to self-defense. In the same spirit with which we amended step 3, we may interpret step 4 as asserting a right to reasonable sorts of self-defense: measures of defending oneself (or others in the household) that do not illegitimately harm others or violate their rights.

Although this, too, may seem obviously correct, it is also questionable. When others are threatening your physical security, certain measures may be necessary to protect your security. That's self-evident. But it does not follow that *you* have a right to take those protective measures if some other party has appropriately assumed responsibility for taking them on your behalf. As Hobbes argued centuries ago, when we leave "the state of nature" and enter civil society, which features government rule rather than anarchy and rampant vigilantism, we transfer some of our rights to a government whose job description includes protecting us from various well-known types of threats, including others' willingness to do us violence.[2] The police, an arm of the government, are permitted to chase down villains, apprehend them (forcibly, if necessary), and bring them to jail to await trial. We, as individual private citizens, generally lack the authority to do these things. Therefore, it is a significant question whether our basic right to physical security grounds not just a right *that reasonable measures be taken* to protect that basic right from being violated but also a right *to take those measures oneself.* If the right to take those measures oneself, which one presumably has outside civil society, has been *delegated* to the police and, in the case of foreign threats, to the military, then our basic right to physical security does *not* ground a broad right of self-defense.

Yet surely, even if we Americans have delegated the protection of our physical security to the police and armed forces, we retain *some* right to self-defense. Suppose that during sixth-grade recess Tom starts bullying Jeff without provocation. If there is an understanding that there is to be no fighting, and a supervising adult is able and willing to intervene in such situations, then maybe Jeff has no right to defend himself as the term "self-defense" is usually understood: by fighting back. Perhaps he may only shout to the supervising adult. But it is easy to imagine situations in which protection by others is far less available. In more typical scenarios involving sixth-grade recess (at least as I remember them), a kid cannot always count on effective adult intervention when a bully bullies. In those more typical situations, it seems entirely reasonable that someone who is being bullied has a right to fight back, if doing so appears necessary to thwart the intimidation and assault. So, we may revise step 4 so that it asserts that the qualified right to self-defense is further qualified so that it applies wherever (but only where) self-defense is necessary to prevent one's basic rights from being violated. In the playground scenario, Jeff's self-defense may prove necessary if he cannot rely on effective adult intervention to protect him.

Step 5 states that the right to self-defense includes the freedom to use adequate means to defend oneself. The basic idea is sound. A right to self-defense, even when qualified along the lines just indicated, would not be very meaningful if one were only free to use inadequate means. If we said to prospective bullying victims, "Sure, you may fight back, but you have to use a feather rather than your fists," we would make a mockery of the so-called right we were supposedly affirming. At the same time, we must not forget the relevant qualifications: that there is not another party who has responsibility for protecting one's security and can do so reliably, and that adequate means to self-defense do not involve illegitimately harming or violating the rights of others (as in the example of someone who would have to blow up dozens of innocent people to prevent being assassinated).

The Argument from Physical Security has become subtler and more nuanced in our effort to increase its plausibility. In its qualified form, however, it is plausible—thus far. Before proceeding to the more debatable steps of the argument, let us explicitly formulate the revised APS through step 5:

1. People have a basic right to physical security.
2. This right is violated by (unjustified) assaults and is threatened by burglaries.
3. People have a moral right to take necessary measures to prevent their basic rights from being violated—so long as these measures do not involve illegitimately harming or violating the rights of others.
4. The latter right supports a qualified moral right to self-defense: a right to defend oneself where doing so (1) is necessary to prevent one's basic rights from being violated and (2) does not involve illegitimately harming or violating the rights of others.
5. The qualified moral right to self-defense includes the freedom to use adequate means to defend oneself—provided using such means (1) is necessary to prevent one's basic rights from being violated and (2) does not involve illegitimately harming or violating the rights of others.

EVALUATING THE SECOND HALF OF THE ARGUMENT

The key issues in the first half of the Argument from Physical Security were conceptual and moral rather than empirical. The second half of APS raises difficult empirical questions.

Consider step 6: *In present-day circumstances in the United States, adequate self-defense requires that competent adults have the option of gun ownership.* Limiting the claim's scope to competent adults reflects the commonsense notion that only they can be expected to be able to use guns properly. Also, the claim isn't that *no competent adult* can adequately defend herself without a gun. Maybe some can, say, by threatening intruders with a baseball bat.

Now, recall that the right to self-defense was qualified to situations in which defense of one's security *by others* (e.g., the police) was reasonably expected to be inadequate. APS claims that, for some people in this country, such peaceful means as calling the police are inadequate to protect their physical security. Confronted by an intruder, they may need to *defend themselves actively.* Thus, the claim in step 6 is that many competent adults in the United States can defend themselves adequately only if they possess one or more guns. Is this true?

Many of us who do not own guns achieve a sense of home security by locking doors and any windows that can be opened from outside, being prepared to call the police if someone attempts a break-in, and the like. Some install house alarms; others get noisy dogs who are proficient at alerting you when someone is on the premises. Perhaps these measures of self-defense are sufficient in light of the fact that we, as members of civil society, have delegated much of the work of protecting ourselves to the police, who are armed and trained to handle such situations.

Yet one might doubt the sufficiency of such measures. Aggressive burglars might pick locks, smash through windows, or shoot the family dog. If the aforementioned measures of house protection do not prevent a break-in, what should one do as the best way of protecting oneself and the family? Those of us who do not own guns might do best by calling the police and staying as quiet as possible.

Understandably, many Americans consider such measures inadequate. Thousands of criminals in the United States are already well-armed—a fact that distinguishes this country from some other developed nations. So, even if people secure their houses properly and call the police promptly, such measures may leave them unnecessarily vulnerable in the absence of firepower with which to threaten and possibly shoot intruders, who may be armed. One has a right to use force—if necessary—to repel an intruder and, according to the argument, doing so with adequate means requires the option of gun ownership. This argument has a ring of plausibility.

At the same time, we know that guns are frequently *misused* in the household—for example, in shootings prompted by arguments, impulsive suicides, and gun accidents. Many of the injuries and fatalities that result from such incidents would not have occurred had guns been unavailable. Gun ownership has risks along with whatever protective benefits it offers.

This brings us to a factual question: *Does the option of owning firearms enable more adequate self-defense and physical security than would be possible if this option were unavailable?* If one simply imagines a homeowner using a gun to ward off an intruder, and being incapable of doing so without a gun, it might seem obvious that gun ownership promotes effective self-defense. But, because our question is empirical, the answer should be responsive to evidence.

An even-handed examination of available evidence suggests that, in the United States today, possession of guns *does not*, generally speaking, enable more adequate self-defense and physical security.[3] First, the evidence suggests that owning guns tends to be self-defeating in the sense of making household members, on balance, less safe than they would be if the house were free of firearms. Second, the evidence casts doubt on the proposition that, in the event of a break-in while one is at home, having a gun, on balance, promotes the goal of self-defense.

Consider the point about self-defeat. First, having a gun at home increases one's likelihood of dying by suicide.[4] This is hardly surprising considering that many suicide attempts are impulsive, reflecting immediate stressors rather than long-term hopelessness,[5] and that guns used at close range are highly likely to kill rather than merely injure. Second, the risk of death by homicide is considerably greater in homes with guns than in homes without guns.[6] In homes with domestic violence, the chances that such violence will prove lethal are much higher if guns are present.[7] The risk of accidental death also increases markedly in households with guns.[8] On the whole, having guns at home increases the risk of household members' suffering a violent death.[9] Thus, owning guns for the purpose of self-defense is apparently self-defeating in this sense: *Household members, on average, face a greater chance of suffering a violent death if the house contains one or more guns than if the house is free of firearms.*

Before proceeding with the analysis, it is worth noting a consistent pattern among gun fatalities in the United States for at least the last several decades: More than half of the fatalities are suicides.[10] Some gun advocates are likely to challenge any assumption that suicides are, like homicides, bad results that should count as gun tragedies. The basis for this challenge is the idea that a competent adult has a right to take his own life. In response, I do not dispute the idea that some suicides are autonomous acts that may represent the individuals' best option under very difficult circumstances. At the same time, I believe that I have the backing of common sense in maintaining that many or most suicides are tragic events. Relatedly, many suicides are not autonomous actions performed by competent adults. Some people who commit suicides are minors. Others are mentally ill adults who, at their baseline of mental health, would not prefer suicide. Still others are individuals who, whether mentally ill or not, commit suicide impulsively with a weapon that can kill with a simple trigger pull. Only those suicides that are performed by competent adults after careful, well-informed consideration of their options—and not impulsively—are even *candidates* for autonomous suicides. To sweep the large number of suicides under the same legitimating cover of respect for autonomy is to hide some of the evidence of guns' dangerousness in households.

Returning to our analysis, we see that household members, on average, face a greater chance of suffering a violent death if the house contains one or more guns. In this way gun ownership tends not to be an effective means of protecting physical security in the household. Notice that this could be true without contradicting the claim that, *in the event of a break-in when one is home*, having a firearm is the most effective means of self-defense. Many gun owners—and many people who do not own guns—never find themselves in this situation. But it is worth considering whether gun ownership is effective for those who do. Once again, we should consider evidence rather than simply using our imaginations and making assumptions.

Unfortunately, there is not much evidence bearing directly on the matter. Some evidence mixes cases involving encounters with burglars in the home and cases involving encounters with would-be robbers or assailants outside the home. David Hemenway summarizes the data: "[V]ictims appear no more likely to be injured once they threaten the criminal with any weapon [not necessarily a gun], or call the police. . . . In addition, other data suggest that while resisting with a gun might reduce the chance of being injured, it increases the likelihood of being killed. . ."[11] Regarding self-defense with weapons other than a gun, Hemenway cites a set of national surveys that found "more incidents of successful self-defense with a baseball bat than with a firearm."[12] With such limited data, we cannot draw confident conclusions about the effectiveness of using a gun for self-defense in an actual encounter in the home. But it seems fair to say that proponents of APS cannot claim to have strong empirical support for the proposition that the option of gun ownership is necessary for adequate self-defense in the home in the United States today.

Doubts about the effectiveness of gun ownership as a means of self-defense in the home may increase when one considers the uncertainty homeowners sometimes face in deciding whether a particular situation truly requires self-defense. Guns are more lethal than baseball bats, knives, and, of course, less violent measures such as calling the police or simply hiding. Because of guns' lethality, false positives—instances in which a homeowner mistakenly believes that someone on the premises is an intruder—can be especially tragic. One famous case involved a Japanese exchange student who identified the wrong house for a Halloween party and approached the door after the homeowner shouted "Freeze!" (possibly because the student thought he heard "Please!"). The homeowner fatally shot the student.[13] A recent case involved a man whose fiancée alerted him that someone was incessantly banging on the front door. The man got his gun, exited his house from the back, and approached the would-be intruder. The latter, an elderly man with dementia, approached the homeowner, who shot him dead.[14] It is tragic in these and similar cases that innocent, nondangerous persons were killed owing to being mistaken for criminals. In the two cases just described, the tragedy is compounded by the fact that the homeowners could have simply stayed inside, locked their doors, and hurt no one.

Let us take stock before resuming our analysis of APS. Does the point that gun ownership is generally self-defeating invalidate APS by destroying the credibility of step 6? Although I am inclined to believe so, I recognize that I lack a "knock-down" argument. A gun advocate might emphasize that gun owners differ. Some are more cautious, and less impulsive, than others. Some gun owners live in more dangerous neighborhoods than others. Even if gun ownership is self-defeating *on average across the American population*—as available evidence suggests—it may not be self-defeating for everyone. There may be individuals for whom gun ownership is not self-defeating, and maybe they can know this about themselves. If so, they might reasonably assert a right to own firearms as a reasonable means of realizing their right to physical security. Moreover, one might argue, the law should not try to discriminate between those who are and those who are not in such a position, so the law should recognize a right to gun ownership among competent, law-abiding adults. So let us consider it an open question whether APS establishes a moral right to gun ownership among competent adults in the United States today, as asserted by the intermediate conclusion stated in step 7.

Assume, for argument's sake, that there is such a right. As discussed in chapter 10, rights are limited in scope and may sometimes be overridden. A right to gun ownership would be limited in scope by restricting it to competent, law-abiding adults.[15] Only competent adults can be assumed to be able to handle guns properly. And only those who qualify as law-abiding can be entrusted to do so rather than engaging in criminal activities with guns. (In the final chapter, we will consider what is to count as law-abiding and how to assess competence in the relevant sense.) Within its scope, a right may "prevail" or it may be defeated—overridden— by appeal to the public welfare or conflicting rights. Step 8 asserts that the present right is not overridden by either of these considerations among competent, law-abiding adults, an assumption that leads to the assertion in step 9 that the moral right to gun ownership should enjoy legal backing. But is the assumption in step 8 correct?

In approaching this question, consider a respectable case in favor of this assumption:

> *Case in Favor.* The right to gun ownership is a negative right—a right of noninterference—and negative rights are not to be swept away in the tide of appeals to the public welfare. Consider, by way of analogy, the right to freedom from torture. Suppose local police decide that gang violence around town could be reduced with more

information about gang leaders' identities, methods, and plans. The police plausibly believe they can acquire this information by capturing a few gang members and torturing them until they supply what is wanted. If rights could be justifiably set aside in the name of societal benefit, then torturing gang members could easily be justified: however awful the torture is a for a few people, the harms of gang violence that could be prevented by using information gathered through torture are much greater. But to torture the gang members would be a grotesque violation of their rights, a violation that is not justified by appeal to the public interest. Negative rights are moral side constraints. They can be overridden, if at all, only rarely and in extreme situations—such as a genuine ticking-bomb scenario, which might justify torture—but the public harms associated with high rates of gun ownership do not constitute such an emergency. The right to own guns must be protected by law.[16]

This is a strong argument. Because many gun advocates seem to think along these lines, even gun opponents should be able to understand why advocates are often confident about their position. Assuming there is a moral right to gun ownership, the argument just presented invokes a widely accepted understanding of the power of negative rights to resist appeals to utility. Yet, despite these indications of promise, I reject Case in Favor.

My reasons for rejecting this argument are developed in two later chapters, in which I present a consequentialist case for gun control and a rights-based case, respectively. Here I will indicate the general direction of those later arguments. In chapter 13, I emphasize the devastating consequences of widespread gun ownership in a societal context in which gun regulations are minimal. I develop the argument, first, by reminding the reader of how much more likely household members are to die a violent death if the house contains one or more guns than if the house is firearm free. Next, I present evidence indicating the harm to society associated with widespread gun ownership in a context of minimal gun control. The evidence, I argue, is overwhelming—and the harmful consequences are massive, so massive that it is unclear that a negative right to gun ownership would—as Case in Favor claims—prevail over appeal to these consequences.

In chapter 14, I consider the possibility that APS is correct in claiming that the negative right to gun ownership prevails over appeals to societal consequences. Now, a reasonable person might judge that for me to acknowledge this possibility is to give too little weight to societal consequences while accepting an implausibly strict conception of negative rights. That may be true, but I will not rest my case on this claim. Instead, I develop a rights-based case for gun control that succeeds even if we grant the gun advocate's claim: that the pernicious social consequences of gun ownership do not justify overriding the negative right to gun ownership. My rights-based case for gun control has two components.

First, I emphasize that negative rights are meaningless unless they are *enforced*. Because negative rights include the right of innocent people *not to be shot*—a right derived from other more general rights such as rights not to be assaulted and not to be killed—the right not to be shot needs to be enforced. But enforcement includes taking reasonable measures to prevent innocent people from being shot. So, the right to own guns and the right not to be shot have to be specified in awareness of one another, as it were. If there is a utility-trumping negative right to gun ownership, it should not be overturned by a gun ban to support a right not to be shot. By the same token, the right not to be shot should not be ignored by taking the right to own guns to preclude gun control. Gun control is compatible with gun ownership rights and merely limits the scope of gun rights by reasonably enforcing the right not to be shot.

My second rights-based argument asserts, citing plausible examples, a right to a reasonably safe environment. This right is in tension with gun ownership rights. The two rights are compatible, but specifications of their scope must take each other into account. In parallel fashion to the consequentialist argument, this rights-based argument vindicates gun control.

Where does this leave us in terms of our evaluation of APS? APS is in serious trouble. To see why, let's walk through the remaining steps.

Step 6 claims that in the United States today adequate self-defense requires competent adults to have the option of owning guns. But, since the first half of APS needed revisions to retain plausibility, step 6 also needs modification. Appropriately revised, step 6 in effect incorporates three subclaims—*all of which are open to serious challenge*. First, as already discussed, step 6 claims that having a gun is an *effective* means of promoting self-defense and, ultimately, physical security. This claim, again, is challenged by evidence suggesting that gun ownership tends to undermine physical security. The revised step 6 must also claim that self-defense is *necessary* for the protection of physical security. This claim is put in doubt by the availability of police protection and the absence of compelling evidence that gun ownership improves one's odds in the event of an encounter with an intruder. Finally, step 6 must claim that gun ownership *does not illegitimately harm or violate the rights of others*. This is put in doubt by evidence for the self-defeating nature of gun ownership—the way it increases risk of injury and death to household members—as well as evidence presented in chapter 13 concerning harm to members of society, and arguments presented in chapter 14 suggesting that gun ownership (unless properly regulated) routinely violates the rights of other household members, perhaps especially children.

As mentioned earlier, I tend to believe that the problems facing step 6 undermine APS. But I also believe there is a sympathetic way of looking at this step that prevents it from being decisively refuted. In this more sympathetic vein, we may judge that, *for some individuals*, gun ownership is an effective means of self-defense and is not self-defeating, is needed because police protection cannot reasonably be relied upon, and does not illegitimately harm others or violate their rights. Because all this is true for some people in our country, the reasoning continues, the *option* of gun ownership must be available to competent adults. Otherwise, the state, in making gun ownership illegal, would wrongly interfere with some people's (qualified) right to self-defense and their basic right to physical security.

While this sympathetic construal of step 6 keeps the argument for gun rights alive, it cannot possibly support a conclusion that opposes gun control, as we are about to see. On the basis of the fragile step 6, step 7 asserts that competent adults in the United States have a moral right to gun ownership. But how could all competent adults have this right? It is only true of some competent adults that their situation fits the three subclaims of step 6 just discussed. APS is more plausible if we restrict the scope of those who have the moral right much more narrowly than the set of all competent adults—that is, all adults who do not count as incompetent for reasons of documented substantial mental illness, mental retardation, or the like. An appropriate scope would be those competent adults who (1) can be counted on not to defeat themselves (or their families) in terms of physical security by owning guns, (2) genuinely need guns because police protection cannot reasonably be relied upon or because of an especially dangerous occupation, and (3) do not illegitimately threaten to harm or violate the rights of others through gun possession. Assuming only those who actually have a moral right to own guns should be legally entitled to obtain one, this raises the question of how to identify the right individuals. And here we may cut to the chase: only gun control regulations beyond what most American gun advocates find palatable could identify the individuals who have the relevant right. For one thing, in order to identify those individuals, the state would have to restrict gun ownership to those who can demonstrate (or have a third party demonstrate) that they have genuine need—a restriction that is a major piece of gun control. Among this group, the state would have to make reasonable efforts to restrict gun ownership to those who can be trusted to store and use guns safely, so that their gun ownership is neither self-defeating in terms of physical security nor illegitimately threatening to the well-being or rights of others. This would require gun safety and use training, another major piece of gun control.

There is no need to belabor the remainder of APS. Note, however, that we have not even considered step 8, that the moral right to own guns is not overridden by other considerations. In chapter 13, we will find some reason to believe that it is, in fact, overridden by consequentialist considerations. But this line of argument is far from certain and I will not endorse it. Even if APS securely reaches the conclusion that the moral right should enjoy legal protection, as step 9 claims, it could never safely reach the anti-gun control shores of step 10. As even the gun-friendly majority of the Supreme Court acknowledged, gun rights are compatible with gun control.

APS cannot justify opposition to gun control. Is it possible that some similar argument can prove more successful? Although I consider APS the strongest argument that appeals to physical security or self-defense, I can imagine two similar arguments that might be thought to provide a stronger basis for gun rights. One variation claims that a right to self-defense is basic and does not depend on the role of self-defense in protecting physical security. This approach might avoid APS's vulnerability to the charge that gun ownership tends to make one, on balance, less physically secure. Another version claims, somewhat similarly, that one has a right, grounded in dignity or self-respect, "to go down fighting," rendering irrelevant any evidence suggesting that one is better off—in terms of expected outcomes—simply calling the police. Each of these alternatives, I think, faces several problems that cast doubt on its ability to support gun rights. But, even if I am wrong about this, these variations on APS could never serve as a rational basis for opposing gun control. People can have a right to gun ownership and exercise this right with considerable latitude even if their state imposes moderately extensive regulations in order to promote public safety and law enforcement. I conclude that appeals to self-defense and physical security do not justify opposition to gun control.

NOTES

1. The present formulation improves the one stated in my "Handguns, Moral Rights, and Physical Security," *Journal of Moral Philosophy* 1 (2014): 56–76. The evaluation of the argument that follows borrows ideas from the earlier article while substantially modifying and expanding upon the earlier discussion.
2. Thomas Hobbes, *Leviathan* (1651).
3. Nicholas Dixon reaches the same conclusion in "Handguns, Philosophers, and the Right to Self-Defense," *International Journal of Applied Philosophy* 25 (2011): 151–70.
4. See D. A. Brent et al., "The Presence and Accessibility of Firearms in the Homes of Adolescent Suicides: A Case-Controlled Study," *JAMA* 266 (1991): 2989–95; Arthur Kellermann et al., "Suicide in the Home in Relation to Gun Ownership," *New England Journal of Medicine* 327 (1992): 467–72; Antoine Chapdelaine and Pierre Maurice, "Firearms Injury Prevention and Gun Control in Canada," *Canadian Medical Association Journal* 155 (1996): 1285–89; Yeats Conwell, Kenneth Connor, and Christopher Cox, "Access to Firearms and Risk for Suicide in Middle-Aged and Older Adults," *American Journal of Geriatric Psychiatry* 10 (2002): 407–16; Matthew Miller, Deborah Azrael, and David Hemenway, "Firearm Availability and Unintentional Firearm Deaths, Suicide, and Homicide Among 5–14 Year Olds," *Journal of Trauma Injury, Infection, and Critical Care* 52 (2002): 267–75; and Matthew Miller and David Hemenway, "Guns and Suicide in the United States," *New England Journal of Medicine* 359 (2008): 989–91. For a recent

meta-analysis, see Andrew Anglemyer, Tara Horvath, and George Rutherford, "The Accessibility of Firearms and Risk for Suicide and Homicide Victimization Among Household Members: A Systematic Review and Meta-Analysis," *Annals of Internal Medicine* 160, no. 2 (2014): 101–13.

5. Thomas Simon, Alan Swann, Kenneth Powell, et al., "Characteristics of Impulsive Suicide Attempts and Attempters," *Suicide and Life-Threatening Behavior* 32 (suppl.) (2002): 49–59.

6. See A. L. Kellermann et al., "Gun Ownership as a Risk Factor for Homicide in the Home," *New England Journal of Medicine* 329 (1993): 1084–91; Miller, Azrael, and Hemenway, "Firearm Availability and Unintentional Firearm Deaths,"; D. J. Wiebe, "Homicide and Suicide Risks Associated with Firearms in the Home: A National Case-Control Study," *Annals of Emergency Medicine* 41 (2003): 771–82; and Anglemyer, Harvath, Rutherford, et al., "The Accessibility of Firearms."

7. See L. E. Saltzman et al., "Weapon Involvement and Injury Outcomes in Family and Intimate Assaults," *JAMA* 267 (1992): 3043–47; and J. C. Campbell et al., "Risk Factors for Femicide in Abusive Relationships: Results from a Multisite Case Control Study," *American Journal of Public Health* 93 (2003): 1089–97.

8. See Matthew Miller and David Hemenway, "Firearm Availability and Unintentional Firearm Deaths," *Accident Analysis & Prevention* 33 (2001): 477–84; and D. J. Wiebe, "Firearms in U.S. Homes as a Risk Factor for Unintentional Gunshot Fatality," *Accident Analysis and Prevention* 35 (2003): 711–16.

9. Garen Wintemute, "Guns, Fear, the Constitution, and the Public's Health," *New England Journal of Medicine* 358 (2008): 1421–24.

10. Drew Desilver, "Suicides Account for Most Gun Deaths," Pew Research Center webpage, http://www.pewresearch.org/fact-tank/2013/05/24/suicides-account-for-most-gun-deaths/, accessed November 21, 2015.

11. David Hemenway, *Private Guns, Public Health* (Ann Arbor: University of Michigan Press, 2010), 78. Hemenway cites F. E. Zimring and J. Zuehl, "Victim Injury and Death in Urban Robbery: A Chicago Study," *Journal of Legal Studies* 15 (1986): 1–40.

12. Hemenway, *Private Guns, Public Health*, 77. He cites National Crime Victimization Survey, *Crime Victimization 2001* (Washington, DC: Bureau of Justice Statistics, 2001) and Harvard Injury Control Research Center, *Analysis of 1999 National Survey* (Cambridge, MA: Harvard Injury Control Research Center, 2001).

13. The case is described in Wintemute, "Guns, Fear, the Constitution, and the Public's Health," 1421.

14. Ray Henry, "Ga. Man Who Fatally Shot Alzheimer's Patient Won't Be Charged," *Washington Post*, March 1, 2014, A16. For further anecdotes along similar lines, including several involving parents mistakenly killing their own children, see Hemenway, *Private Guns, Public Health*, 70–71, 73–74.

15. Later I will argue for restricting the scope of this putative right considerably further. Here I am presenting reasoning in support of APS.

16. Huemer presents something like this reasoning in "Is There a Right to Own a Gun?"

anyway, don't violate your rights; rather, at least typically, they circumscribe your liberty and specific rights. It is not as if people have a right to enter my house without permission, but this right is *overridden* or *violated* by my rights to property and physical security, which forbid entry without my permission. Similarly, it is not as if you have a right to swing your knuckles into my nose, but this right is overridden or violated by my right to physical security. Rather, in each case the morally protected liberty or right is circumscribed so that it does not include the prohibited action. The scope of morally protected liberties is generally limited by other people's rights and the requirement that one not intentionally or negligently harm other people.

In reply, one might claim that there is no significant difference between (1) my assertion that rights protecting liberty are restricted in scope in ways suggested by the above two examples and (2) the assertion that there is a general, unrestricted right to liberty, which is overridden by other people's rights and the importance of not harming others. To be sure, what is asserted in (2) is not logically incoherent, and perhaps not subject to decisive refutation. But the picture offered by (2) suggests enormously capacious rights that are constantly contradicting each other. And since rights, by their nature (see chapter 10), are generally not supposed to be violated or overridden, this picture suggests a need for massive, continual regret for the way in which my property rights and right to bodily integrity override your capacious, general right to liberty. Intuitively, it doesn't seem that I have any reason for regret here. So I am confident in suggesting that it is far more perspicuous and sensible to understand rights as limited *in their scope* by other rights. I am nearly as confident that it makes more sense to speak of specific liberty rights rather than a general right to liberty. In any case, I will speak of specific liberty rights such as freedom of speech and freedom of religion. Three such specific freedoms will be at issue in rights claims that serve as challenges to gun control.

THE ASSERTION OF A BASIC RIGHT TO OWN GUNS

Some American gun advocates claim that there is a *basic* or *fundamental* right to own guns. Clearly the asserted right is a liberty right or right of noninterference—a right to freedom to own a gun, not a positive right or entitlement to be provided with a gun. What is most interesting in the present claim, but also somewhat unclear, is the assertion that the right is basic.

Philosophers and legal scholars understand basic rights in somewhat different ways, but they generally have in mind rights that are general and foundational rather than specific and derived from more general rights. In chapter 10, I endorsed the conception of basic rights according to which they are *moral rights whose fulfillment (1) protects highly general interests that are vital to the prospects for having a reasonably healthy, active life of normal length and (2) is needed for one's enjoyment of rights generally.* The basic right at the center of chapter 11's analysis was the right to physical security. If one's physical security is frequently threatened by attempted assault, rape, homicide, or the like, one does not have good prospects for a long, healthy life. And, without physical security, it is extremely difficult to exercise other rights such as the right to vote, the right to an education, and the right to peaceful assembly. Moreover, physical security is a highly general good. For these reasons, a right to physical security is plausibly regarded as basic, according to the present conception of basic rights.

From this perspective, a claim that a right to gun ownership is basic seems unsustainable. For one thing, it's not true that having the freedom to own guns is vital to the prospects for a long, healthy life. Even in the United States, which is awash with guns, most of the people I know who have had long, healthy lives have not owned guns. In fairness to the present claim, however, the assertion is that *the freedom to own guns* is the object of the basic right, not *actually owning* them; one may have this freedom without exercising it. At the same time, when I think of most people I know in the United States—and, for that matter, virtually everyone I know in Canada, Europe, Japan, Australia, and other developed countries—it does not seem that freedom to own a gun has played any significant role in their having long, healthy lives. Nor, speaking for myself and people I know, does the freedom to own guns seem a necessary condition to enjoying other rights. My ability to enjoy my rights to freedom of movement, freedom of expression, freedom to work, education, and even physical security have not required my having the option of buying and keeping a gun. In fairness to gun proponents, however, I must acknowledge that I and most of the people with whom I associate enjoy the relatively safe existence of life in the American middle or upper-middle classes. And some of my associates enjoy the safer, less violence-plagued existence of life in developed countries other than the United States.

One can imagine my opponent emphasizing different circumstances in which Americans find themselves and contending that some members of our society need guns for the enjoyment of other rights and for a reasonable prospect for a long, healthy life. Is this true? We found in chapter 11 that, for the most part, Americans enjoy *less* physical security—and, specifically, face a greater chance of dying a violent death—if they live in a household with at least one gun than if they live in a gun-free household. But there are probably exceptions to this statistical generalization. For example, gun owners who cannot count on police to provide adequate protection and are especially careful with gun storage and use may enjoy a net gain in safety from gun ownership (and therefore from the freedom to own guns).

But, whereas the last point may play an important role in defending a right to own guns—as discussed in chapter 11—it does not strengthen the case for a *basic* right to gun ownership. At least in the status quo of American gun policy (featuring very minimal gun control), freedom to purchase a gun is not vital to the prospects of living a long, healthy life or enjoying other rights—and is, in fact, at least slightly detrimental to these goals—for most people. To qualify as a basic right, the object of the right must be vital in these ways for most people, not only in exceptional cases.

Furthermore, to make a conceptual point, the right to own guns seems too specific to be a basic right. Basic rights protect *highly general* interests such as physical security or freedom of expression. The freedom to own a gun is a specification of the freedom to own weaponry, of which guns represent only one type. And freedom to own weaponry is not *intrinsically* valuable, unless one is interested in weapons because one collects them and finds them esthetically pleasing—in which case they need not be useable as weapons. Freedom to own weaponry derives its importance from the value of self-defense, which as we saw in chapter 11, is derivative from our basic right to physical security, or from other, more general freedoms such as the freedom to pursue one's own conception of the good life, as discussed later in this chapter. Gun ownership is too specific, and derived, to count as a basic right.

Now, my opponent might respond that the conceptual argument of the previous paragraph is entirely semantic. She might say that a better, more relevant understanding of basic rights would not require that they protect highly general interests. Rather, what's important about basic rights is their vital role in making possible the enjoyment of other rights and/or a decent chance at a long, healthy life.[2] She might add that sometimes specific rights derived from highly general rights are just as important as the latter. For example, assuming children have a right not to be negligently exposed to things that will kill them, a child with a deadly allergy to peanuts has a right not to be negligently exposed to peanuts—and this specific, derived right is as morally forceful as the more general right.[3] This is an excellent point. My right not to be involuntarily spray-painted in the face is no less significant, and no more liable to overriding for being specific, than my more general right not to be assaulted. Let us therefore assume, for a moment, that the fact that gun ownership rights might be derived from more general rights does not preclude the possibility that they are basic—or, more to the point, just as morally important as the more general right, such as self-defense or physical security, from which they derive.

The problem for my opponent is that the relationship between the freedom to purchase guns and physical security is not at all like the relationship between the allergic child's need to avoid peanut butter and his need to live. If he has peanut butter, he will almost certainly die. In contrast, it is simply false that not having the option of owning guns virtually guarantees a loss of physical security.

At the same time, I have acknowledged that there are probably some people in our society who would stand to gain, on balance, in terms of physical security if they had the option of gun ownership. What about them? First, never mind whether we call their right to gun ownership basic. To me, it seems to misuse language to do so, but that again is just a semantic point. Let us assume, for argument's sake, that these individuals have a moral right to gun ownership and, indeed, such a right that is not overridden by appeal to public safety or other rights. What follows?

From the standpoint of gun control, nothing follows that the opponent of gun control will welcome. Indeed, as we saw in chapter 11, the only way to have any reasonable idea who is likely to enjoy a net benefit from gun ownership *requires gun control*: the requirement of a license to own guns contingent upon passing a rigorous safety course, safe storage requirements, and the like. The only way to make it likely that particular gun owners will enhance, rather than threaten, their physical security is to implement appropriate sorts of gun control. Thus, while some variant of the assertion of a basic right to own guns might help in developing a strong case for gun ownership rights, it appears to have no chance of strengthening an argument against gun control.

But let's consider one last objection from a proponent of the basic-right approach. He may claim that my interpretation of this approach unfairly tethers it to an appeal to physical security, missing the point. The point is that the right to own guns *really is basic* and therefore does not depend on the way in which guns can promote physical security or any other interest more general than gun ownership. While claiming that gun ownership rights are basic in this sense is consistent with what we ordinarily mean by "basic"—fundamental rather than derivative—it is completely implausible. There is nothing intrinsically valuable about guns, unless, again, one regards them as objects of esthetic value, in which case there is no need to be able to fire them. As LaFollette notes, the value of guns is a matter of what we can do with them.[4] If they were useless for shooting people, animals, or targets, they would have no special value *as guns* (as opposed to ornaments or paperweights). Gun proponents are not interested in guns independently of the possibility of firing them. For this reason, we cannot take seriously the claim that their value is irreducible. Instead, we must consider their particular legitimate purposes. One purpose, self-defense, has been considered at length. In the remainder of this chapter, we will consider two other, liberty-related purposes.

THE APPEAL TO FREEDOM TO PURSUE ONE'S OWN CONCEPTION OF THE GOOD LIFE

One strategy for opposing gun control appeals to a right to freedom to pursue one's own conception of the good life. This freedom is central to liberal political visions. By "liberal" here, I do not mean—in the terms of American political discourse—more Democratic than Republican but, rather, *liberty-loving.* This sense of "liberal" includes both socially permissive Democrats and libertarian-leaning Republicans on the American scene. Chief opponents include religious fundamentalists, socialists, and, to some extent, communitarians. Liberal political visions in the present sense embrace pluralism with respect to lifestyles and conceptions of the good life. The assertion in the Declaration of Independence of a right to the pursuit of happiness may be understood as positing the right to freedom to pursue one's own conception of the good life. Acceptance of this right is nearly universal in Western societies.

Like the opponent of gun control, I accept that there is some such right—even if, as with all general rights, its scope must be circumscribed. How does this right bear on the ethics of gun ownership? It does so by underwriting a variety of presumably legitimate activities, each of which involves guns. Let us consider four such activities: target shooting, gun collecting, hunting, and membership in gun-centered clubs.

Target shooting is a perfectly legitimate activity, assuming reasonable precautions are taken to limit associated risks. On an autobiographical note, the only time I have used guns was during target shooting at Boy Scouts summer camp. The instructors took great care to minimize the possibility of harm and, as I remember, there was nothing problematic about the shooting practice. Campers shot guns and no one was put at risk. I enjoyed myself. Target shooting seems to me the sort of activity that should be available to people who can be expected to participate safely. Then those whose vision of satisfying recreation includes target shooting will be able to participate. But target shooting is not inconsistent with gun control. It is only reasonable to insist on certain precautions—in effect, forms of gun control—that reduce the likelihood of harm. For example, if children engage in target shooting, supervision by adults should be mandatory. I would also favor a requirement that the adults who are to supervise demonstrate competence in the handling of guns. Although such a requirement would pose some inconvenience to the adults in question, and perhaps to children who are eager to participate, the legitimate societal interest in safety can support such a requirement while leaving intact a right, albeit a qualified or limited right, to use guns in target shooting.

An interesting aspect of this activity, unlike self-defense in the home, it that it does not require gun *ownership on the part of private individuals* (as opposed to private clubs or businesses that make target shooting available). A right to engage in target shooting could be enjoyed even if there were no gun ownership by private citizens. The activity could be restricted to target-shooting clubs, camps, and ranges, which could lend guns to club members or paying customers, subject to regulations that are reasonably related to safety.

Contrast the activity of gun collecting. One cannot collect guns without owning them. Gun aficionados may claim, plausibly, that their vision of the good life includes collecting these items of fascination and that, so long as gun collectors do not harm or pose unreasonable risks to others, they should be able to purchase and own guns in pursuit of this hobby. Interestingly, while gun collecting, unlike target shooting, requires the freedom to *own* guns, collecting guns, unlike target shooting, does not require the freedom to *fire* guns. One can collect to one's heart's delight without ever using a gun in the standard sense of firing it. So, this particular activity, understood as an instance of exercising the freedom to pursue one's own conception of the good life, can support a right to own guns but not to fire them. Other legitimate activities such as self-defense may support the right to use guns in some circumstances, but it is important to decouple any prerogative to collect guns from a prerogative to use them. One could imagine a protected legal right to own highly dangerous, historically significant firearms—such as machine guns—along with a reasonable legal requirement *not* to own or possess the ammunition that they are capable of firing. Such a restriction, of course, would constitute a type of gun control.

While target shooting and gun collecting may not require rights both to own and to use the relevant guns, a protected right to hunt would obviously include the right to use the weapons, and it is hard to imagine hunters' not being able to own them as well. But the ethics of hunting is fairly complicated. For one thing, it cannot avoid the complex issue of animals' moral status, for if animals have significant moral status, then it hardly makes sense to regard them as targets for recreational hunting. Now, animals' having significant moral status would not automatically preclude hunting for the purpose of culling deer populations or hunting for food. Yet, other difficult issues would arise. For example, are there less violent yet feasible ways of controlling deer populations, such as sterilization programs? Is hunting for food justified if one can obtain adequate nourishment without doing so? Fortunately, our purposes do not require diving into these thickets of moral and factual complexity. Instead, we may assume for the sake of argument that some types of hunting fall under the penumbra of activities protected by the liberal value of freedom to pursue one's conception of the good life—*while noting that the right to hunt is compatible with appropriate gun control*. Such gun control might include a requirement of passing a safety course in order to obtain a license to hunt, a limit on what sorts of firearms can be used to hunt, minimum age requirements, and similar measures.

Another activity that might seem to pose a challenge to gun control is membership in gun-centered clubs. Consider someone whose conception of the good life includes membership in a sort of mobster's nostalgia club. Let us assume that members love the tough-guy image of mobsters and prize freedom from government control. Now, for the present argument to be reasonable, we must assume that the club members accept appropriate laws as forms of government control; otherwise, we are imagining people who prefer a Hobbesian state of nature, utter anarchy, to life in a civilized society featuring a government that includes a police force, army, courts, and other institutions of at least a minimal state.[5] Let us consider the challenge that emerges if we take up this observation from Todd Hughes and Lester Hunt: "There are many people . . . whose conception of the good life involves owning, shooting, and training with automatic weapons."[6]

By now it is obvious that a right to freedom to pursue one's own conception of the good life is compatible with some forms of gun control. And we noted early in this book that opposition to all gun control would be crazy. No one could seriously argue, for example, that the right in question encompasses complete freedom from any safety-based restrictions whatsoever or a prerogative of young children to own guns. At most, the present sort of argument can oppose gun control of the relatively extensive sort that I defend. The appeal to the right to pursue one's conception of the good life by joining a gun-centered club challenges a gun control advocate like me by making a case for allowing ownership and limited use of some very dangerous types of weapon. Hughes and Hunt suggest that automatic firearms might fall under the scope of weapons that should be covered by the present argument. By contrast, I defend a ban on automatic and semiautomatic weapons along with high-capacity ammunition clips. Is my position sustainable given the plausible liberal assertion of a right to freedom to pursue one's own vision of the good life?

The issue concerns the scope of this right. The chief justification for limiting the scope appeals to public safety. This appeal justifies, for example, the prohibition of any club whose activities involve use of extremely dangerous weapons such as nuclear arms, dynamite, bazookas, and grenades. Is there a principled way of drawing a line between weapons that are too dangerous to include within the scope of the right in question and weapons that are not too dangerous?

Hughes and Hunt think so. They appeal to the idea of a precision instrument:

> In the relevant respect, guns are as different from dynamite as can be imagined. Like clocks, guns are [with certain exceptions such as sawed-off shotguns] precision instruments: they are designed to function precisely, and for more or less the same reasons that clocks are. People have clocks so that they will know exactly what time it is, and not approximately what

time it is. Similarly, they have guns so they will be able to hit a target, and not nearby objects. The function of a gun is not simply to provide lethal force, but to provide precisely controlled lethal force. Partly because of this fact, it is a surprisingly simple matter to handle a gun safely. As millions of Americans know from their firearm safety training, there are a few easy-to-follow rules that, if they are followed, will guarantee that unplanned detonations will not occur.[7]

Does the distinction between guns that are and those that are not precision instruments provide a defensible basis for delineating the scope of firearms to be included within a right to own and use guns?

No. The question of whether a particular weapon *can* be used precisely and properly is not the only relevant consideration. That a firearm is a precision instrument, in other words, is a necessary but insufficient condition for its being the sort of weapon people should be allowed to own and use. For another relevant question is whether the legal availability of the type of firearm in question poses acceptable or unacceptable risks to the public.

Let us consider the idea that the right to pursue one's own vision of the good life would include a prerogative to own and use automatic firearms in gun-centered clubs such as the mobster's nostalgia club just described. To begin, it is hard for me to think of a gun that keeps firing for as long as you depress the trigger as a precision instrument. Certainly this sort of weapon is enormously dangerous. Even if, in some sense, it qualifies as a precision instrument, we must realistically evaluate the various possible ways of making automatic weapons available to the public.

The most liberal policy (in the present sense of "liberty loving") would be to make them available to competent adults generally, so that those who want to use them in clubs can do so as they please. But a policy this liberal would make it easy not only for club members but also those with criminal intent to have easy access to these weapons. From any sensible standpoint, this is an unacceptable result.

Another possibility would be to allow only those who demonstrate a "need" for such weapons—say, by documenting membership in a gun-centered club—to purchase them. This approach might be safer, but it still seems quite risky to allow any private citizens to buy such dangerous weapons. Certainly it would be easy for people to join special groups, purchase automatic guns, and then sell them on a black market to criminals and fanatical vigilantes.

A more sensible approach would be to allow the group members to use these firearms in private, carefully secured areas without owning them. The law could restrict private ownership of such weapons to registered clubs, which would be required to keep the weapons on the club's premises. This option would seem better from the standpoint of public safety than permitting individuals to own such dangerous firearms.

Another option would be to have restrictions that make it illegal even to *fire* one of these weapons, anywhere. Group members could roam around with unloaded automatic weapons and engage in the same make-believe as they would normally engage in; they just couldn't have ammunition, or automatic weapons that are capable of firing. A more restrictive option, of course, and the one that approximates the American policy status quo (see chapter 9, note 10), is simply not to allow private citizens to own or use these weapons. This approach could respect the right to freedom to pursue one's vision of the good life while noting that this right, like other rights, has limits.

These weapons, I suggest, are just too dangerous to allow in private hands. Although our laws cannot entirely prevent private citizens from gaining access to these and other highly dangerous weapons, since there will always be law-breakers and black markets, our legal system can at least do its part by not encouraging a market in automatic weapons. This, I think, is by far the most sensible approach.

What about semi-automatic weapons, which, although requiring a trigger pull for each shot, can be fired repeatedly without reloading? These weapons are not reasonably related to the goal of household self-defense, but maybe gun aficionados have a stronger claim on using semi-automatic weapons than on using automatic weapons in pursuing their vision of the good life. Certainly there is a more plausible claim that these guns are precision instruments, because every shot requires a separate trigger pull. If the club members' claim here is compelling, it would seem to be compelling for using these weapons in a protected area, not for owning them. Moreover, since the club members would not be allowed to shoot any actual person, it is doubtful that they would have any legitimate claim to use semi-automatic weapons *that can actually fire*. It appears, then, that the appeal to freedom to pursue one's own conception of the good life can support, at most, a very limited right to "use" (but not own) semi-automatic weapons.

THE APPEAL TO FREEDOM FROM A TYRANNICAL GOVERNMENT

Gun control proponents and opponents can agree that a government is legitimate only if it enjoys the broad consent of its people. This test of legitimacy demands some form of democracy and rejects tyranny for violating people's right to representative government. Now, it is one thing to reject tyranny and another to say which means of preventing tyranny are acceptable. Many gun advocates believe that private firearm ownership is a legitimate means of preventing tyranny or at least making it less likely. Samuel Wheeler, for example, sees a well-armed public as a safeguard against the possibility that a government will "go rogue," and the importance of this standing defense against public-sector assailants as a major argument against a ban on gun ownership.[8]

Some gun advocates go further and argue that the importance of a well-armed public as a bulwark against a government willing to institute a tyranny justifies opposition not only to a ban on guns but to gun control as well. As Philip Cook and Kristin Goss put the idea (without endorsing it): "A well-armed citizenry is necessary to counterbalance the state and, if liberty so requires, to topple it. A corollary to this tenet is that banning private ownership of guns, *or even simply regulating them*, makes tyranny—even genocide—more likely."[9] But the idea that gun regulations—even moderately extensive gun control of the sort that I advocate—makes tyranny (or genocide) more likely is very far-fetched. Most other developed countries have gun regulations far more extensive than we have, yet all are stable democracies. It is hard to avoid the impression that gun advocates are using a fantasy—the American government, or some part of it such as the armed forces, attempting to impose a tyranny and private citizens heroically fighting them off—as a rationalization for opposing gun control.

Medicare system for the elderly, is unacceptable for moving too far in the direction of tyranny. The present construal of the argument under consideration should be recognized as a piece of rhetorical excess rather than a serious argument. After all, if we overcome the odds in this country and actually implement substantial gun regulations, we will do so by winning the approval of a majority of the House of Representatives, 60 out of 100 members of the Senate (since fewer than that would be vulnerable to a filibuster), and the president. If this took place, it would be an instance of our government overcoming the enormously powerful gun lobby and instituting laws that are favored by most Americans. That, in other words, would be the precise opposite of tyranny: democracy in action.

CONCLUSION

In this chapter, we have considered three appeals to liberties as arguments against gun control: (1) the assertion of a basic right to (be free to) own guns; (2) the appeal to freedom to pursue one's own conception of the good life; and (3) the appeal to freedom from a tyrannical government. None of these arguments proved successful.

NOTES

1. See Jeremy Waldron, *Liberal Rights* (Cambridge: Cambridge University Press, 1993), ch. 2; and James Griffin, *On Human Rights* (Oxford: Oxford University Press, 2008), ch. 9.

2. Cf. Samuel Wheeler, "Gun Violence and Fundamental Rights," *Criminal Justice Ethics* 20 (2001): 19–24.

3. Ibid, 21.

4. Hugh LaFollette, "Gun Control," *Ethics* 110 (2000): 263–81, at 266–67.

5. In other words, we may assume that the club members are libertarians but not anarchists. For two classic works defending libertarianism, see F. A. Hayek, *The Constitution of Liberty* (Chicago: University of Chicago Press, 1960); and Robert Nozick, *Anarchy, State, and Utopia* (New York, Basic Books, 1974).

6. "The Liberal Basis of the Right to Bear Arms," *Public Affairs Quarterly* 14 (2000): 1–25, at 12–13.

7. Ibid, 10.

8. Wheeler, "Gun Violence and Fundamental Rights."

9. Philip J. Cook and Kristin A. Goss, *The Gun Debate* (Oxford: Oxford University Press, 2014), 31, emphasis mine.

10. Wheeler, "Gun Violence and Fundamental Rights," 19

11. Hugh LaFollette, "Controlling Guns," *Criminal Justice Ethics* 20 (2001): 34–39, at 34.

12. Ibid.

The Consequentialist Case
for Gun Control

■ □ ■

THE PREVIOUS TWO CHAPTERS ATTEMPTED to undermine the strongest arguments opposing gun control. Once again, I am using the term *gun control* as shorthand for *moderately extensive gun control*, meaning gun regulations considerably more extensive than exist today in the United States. Chapter 11 confronted the Argument from Physical Security as a basis for gun rights and against gun control. Chapter 12 undermined several liberty-based arguments against gun control. The present chapter and the one that follows present two components of a positive argument for gun control. This chapter advances the consequentialist portion of the positive case.

As noted in chapter 11, some of the empirical considerations that helped to undermine the Argument from Physical Security also contribute to the positive case for gun control. This body of evidence, we found, suggests that owning guns for the sake of self-defense and, more generally, physical security tends to be self-defeating: *on average and on balance, household members are more likely to die a violent death if they live in a home with guns than if they live in a gun-free home.* Moreover, the best prospect for enabling particular households to overcome this gloomy generalization would involve instituting at least some of the sorts of gun regulations that gun advocates generally resist. The empirical case developed in chapter 11, which supports the idea that widespread gun ownership in the absence of significant safety-promoting gun regulations has unacceptable consequences, focused on *safety in the household.* Further development of the consequentialist case for gun control requires broadening our view from households to *society at large.* Thus, the evidence takes into account not only what happens in homes but also what happens "on the street" or in public.

The remainder of this chapter begins with the consequentialist case for gun control from the perspective of the broader society. It then addresses the oft-made claim that gun ownership has significant deterrent effects on prospective criminals—effects that should be taken into account in any responsible evaluation of gun control. The final section considers the possibility that the consequentialist case for gun control really supports a *ban* on private gun ownership.

THE CONSEQUENTIALIST CASE FOR GUN CONTROL: LOOKING BEYOND THE HOUSEHOLD

In making relevant comparisons between different populations, we will compare those that are roughly similar with respect to economic development and stability. So, for example, we will compare the United States to other developed countries and we will compare different states and regions within the United States to each other. We will not compare, for example, the United States and Canada to Haiti and Liberia, a comparison that would introduce so many variables that may be causally related to gun violence as to make inferences unnecessarily complicated.

Let us begin by returning to some data presented in the introductory chapter, data collected by the United Nations on gun homicides in the United States and three other English-speaking, developed nations: Canada, Great Britain (England and Wales), and Australia.[1] In 2003 through 2009, the annual rate of gun homicide per 100,000 population averaged about 3.7 in the United States. In Canada, the rate per 100,000 people averaged just under 0.6. During this same time period, the average rates in Britain and Australia were 0.1 and just under 0.16, respectively. Thus, in comparison with these three developed, English-speaking nations, the American gun homicide rate, per population size, ranged from just over 6 times as great to 37 times as great. Those are remarkable differences in gun homicide rates.

At least two major differences are likely to bear on gun homicide variations between the United States and these other countries. First, the United States has far more guns in private hands per population size. Second, the other countries have far stricter gun regulations. It is helpful, therefore, to keep in mind two distinct questions. First, do higher rates of gun ownership, other things being equal, have worse consequences than lower rates of gun ownership? Second, does weaker gun control (in terms of both the gun regulations on the books and the degree to which they are actually enforced), other things being equal, have worse consequences than stronger gun control? (Note that "other things" in "other things being equal" includes the strength of gun control in the first question and the rates of gun ownership in the second.)

It is no simple matter to disentangle the likely causal effects of gun ownership rates and of the strength of gun control. Nevertheless, on any reasonable interpretation of existing evidence, there is ample reason to believe that the answer to both questions is affirmative, strengthening the consequentialist case for gun control. And it is quite clear that the *combination* of high gun ownership rates and weak gun control has much worse consequences than the *combination* of low rates of gun ownership and strong gun control, as strongly suggested—at least as far as gun homicide is concerned—by the comparative data just presented regarding the four nations. Further support comes from data comparing homicide rates among, for example, 5-to 14-year-olds in the United States and twenty-five other high-income nations (where guns are less prevalent and gun control is stricter). While the *non-gun* homicide rate was just 1.8 times as high in the United States as in the other countries, the *gun* homicide rate was 13.4 times as high.[2] This supports the *gun availability hypothesis*: the more guns are available, other things being equal, the more violent crimes (here, homicide) will be committed. The evidence in the case of homicide is very strong.[3,4] Note that gun availability is a function of both gun ownership rates and the strictness or laxity of gun regulation. This is important because, for example, even if there are a lot of guns around, they may not be available to children if regulations prohibit their use by children and require safe storage of firearms.

At the same time, we must not make the error of regarding gun ownership rates and strength of gun control as entirely independent variables. After all, many gun control measures reduce the number of guns that are privately owned within a given population. Background checks, for example, determine that some prospective buyers are ineligible. Strict eligibility criteria reduce the number of eligible buyers. Limits on the number of guns eligible buyers may purchase in a given time period also tend to reduce the number of guns in a population. These are just a few of many possible examples of how gun controls tend to reduce gun ownership rates. The point is that strength of gun control and gun ownership rates are related insofar as the first variable affects the second. One reason there is such a high rate of gun ownership in the United States is that it is so easy to purchase firearms lawfully. It is also easy to purchase them *unlawfully*, a fact related not only to weak regulations but also to weak enforcement of those on the books. Weak enforcement is an understandable consequence of laws that have crippled law-enforcement efforts of the ATF and police (see chapter 15). That is why I include under gun control measures—in an admittedly expansive sense of "gun control"—strengthening the ATF's and the police's ability to enforce gun laws. In general, stronger gun regulations along the lines I recommend will predictably lower gun ownership rates in this country, both among those who acquire guns legally and those who acquire them criminally. I advocate both *fewer guns and more safety-related restrictions on their acquisition, storage, and use.* The safety-related restrictions are a means to fewer guns and a means to reducing their harmful misuse.

Let us return to the consequentialist case for gun control and consider *gun accidents*. Several facts support the commonsensical idea that, other things being equal, where there are more guns, there are more gun accidents. In an important study conducted before Congress removed the CDC's ability to examine firearms' effects on public health (see chapter 15), the CDC found that American children under the age of 15 are nine times as likely to die from a gun accident as similarly aged children in other developed countries.[5] Consider now a domestic comparison: a study comparing high-gun-ownership states and low-gun-ownership states found that residents from the former states were over ten times as likely to die in a gun accident as residents in the latter states.[6] A recent review of the evidence confirmed what one would expect on the basis of common sense: "[various types of] studies find that where there are more guns and more guns poorly stored, there are more unintentional firearm deaths."[7] Of course, death is not the only bad consequence that can result from a gun accident. Nonfatal gun accidents also inflict major harm. It is noteworthy, therefore, that one reputable study estimated that for every accidental gun fatality, there are thirteen nonfatal gun accidents that are serious enough to bring their victims to hospital emergency departments.[8]

Let us now consider *suicides*, taking into account both international and domestic comparisons. In comparison with other high-income countries, the U.S. adult suicide rate is close to the average rate. But the American suicide rate for children is much higher (1.6 times) than the average rate among these countries, a difference largely explained by a gun suicide rate eight times the average for young people—ages five to fourteen—in

Burglars, for example, might avoid houses where they know guns are kept—and even houses where they think there is a *good chance* that guns are kept. Prospective robbers and other assailants on the street might avoid targets they consider likely to be armed. Or they might decide not to commit the crime at all. If these speculations are correct, then everyone in a particular community could benefit—at least to some extent (whether or not on balance when other consequences are factored in)—from widespread gun ownership and carrying. Even those who do not own or carry guns could benefit, as "free-riders," if criminals are inhibited by the perception that potential victims are too likely to be armed to make a particular crime worth attempting. Some scholars claim that, indeed, widespread gun ownership deters crime, as suggested by the title of John Lott's book, *More Guns, Less Crime.*[15]

The speculation, on its face, is not implausible. If a burglar, robber, rapist, or other criminal is contemplating a crime of this sort, it is rational, other things being equal, to prefer an unarmed target over an armed one. Thus, if the criminal intends to commit such a crime, he has reason—again, other things being equal—to seek a target (a house or a person on the street) who seems less likely to be armed. If, on the other hand, he is only considering the possibility of committing a crime of this sort, he may decide instead to stay within the law. Either way, the inhibition of the criminal would benefit people who are armed or assumed to be armed. And it would provide a reason to encourage people to buy guns, exactly as the gun lobby does, since everyone would be expected to benefit from a general deterrent effect.

Despite the prima facie reasonableness of this speculation, it is not supported by credible evidence.[16] Studies that are sometimes cited in support of a deterrent effect have been found to have serious flaws. Consider, as a prominent example, the aforementioned book by John Lott, who claims to find that gun ownership rates and crime rates are inversely related; hence, "more guns, less crime." In this body of work, gun ownership data were taken from election exit polls in 1988 and 1996. Among the problems with these data were insufficient sample size (fewer than 100 voters in most states), a possibly unrepresentative sample (actual voters, a minority of the adult population), and a change in the gun ownership question posed to voters between the two years. The data appear to support the incredible claim that the gun ownership rate in the United States *increased more than 50 percent between 1988 and 1996*, despite the fact that other surveys indicate no change or a slight decline in gun ownership rates over this period.[17]

If the evidence does not support the deterrence hypothesis, what does it suggest? In his overview of the topic, David Hemenway states the following:

> A more reliable study [than one he had just criticized] used data from the Uniform Crime Reports for all fifty U.S. states for 1977–98 and data from the U.S. National Crime Victimization Survey (NCVS) for 330,000 households for 1994–98. The findings from both analyses were that U.S. counties and states with more guns have higher rates of burglary and higher per capita rates of "hot burglary" (burglary when someone is at home) (Cook and Ludwig 2003). Homes with firearm collections are considered prime targets for burglars.[18]

security. The consequences of private gun ownership are pernicious. The most sensible policy is to allow only police and military personnel to be armed and assign them alone the job of protecting members of the community. As representatives of the government, they are accountable for their use of force and can be held to strict requirements of training, gun storage, and comportment. Private citizens are safer if none of them is allowed to acquire lethal power.[20]

This is a powerful argument for which I have some sympathy. But I do not believe it represents the most defensible position.

The argument is correct that guns are extremely dangerous. Unlike some other products—such as cars—that cause many deaths every year in our country, guns are designed to be efficient in killing or seriously wounding human or animal targets. The argument is also correct that the overall consequences of the American gun status quo are terrible in comparison with the likely consequences of alternatives that lie significantly down the path of gun control. Moreover, the consequences of the status quo may very well be worse than the likely consequences of a complete ban on private gun ownership; although somewhat speculative, I find the speculation plausible. But I do not see how the evidence we have considered supports the proposition that a gun ban would have better overall consequences in the United States than would gun control along the lines I defend. Such gun control will not make guns entirely safe, but they will make their ownership and use safer on average. Fewer guns will be in private hands and much more will be done to keep them out of criminal hands. If gun possession has any benefits when gun control is at its best, these benefits would be lost if guns were banned. What we don't know is whether the harms avoided through a ban would offset the benefits that would result from the availability of guns under an appropriate regime of gun control.

Suppose we made our best effort to project the likely consequences of a gun ban, coupled with vigorous enforcement efforts, perhaps along with a policy of gun confiscation as a rare overriding of people's right to their legally acquired property. Suppose we then compared this projection with a projection of the likely consequences of gun control along the lines I envision. And suppose it turned out that the projected consequences of a ban—or a ban plus confiscation—would be better than those of gun control. On purely consequentialist grounds, we would then have a strong case for a gun ban.

Yet this would not terminate the ethical debate. Ethicists disagree about whether consequentialism is an adequate approach to ethics. Consequentialism evaluates particular actions and policy options on the basis of whether they can be reasonably expected to produce the best overall results. Where there is persisting, reasonable disagreement is on the question of whether some nonconsequentialist considerations must also be taken into account in the ethical evaluation of our actions and policy choices. These nonconsequentialist factors may include considerations of justice and rights. In the present debate, the possible role of rights is especially important.

Many gun advocates believe they have a moral right to gun ownership, even if the right is restricted or qualified in certain ways. As discussed in chapter 10, rights are valid moral claims that protect central interests and ordinarily resist appeals to the common good as grounds for overriding those claims. In other words, if I have a right to X, then ordinarily I may not be deprived of X even if depriving me of X is conducive to the best overall consequences. This is important to the present discussion because, quite arguably, an outright ban on private gun ownership would violate people's qualified right to self-defense and physical security as discussed in chapter 11. There we found that there was a strong case for the following claim: The (qualified) moral right to self-defense includes the freedom to use adequate means to defend oneself—provided using such means (1) is necessary to prevent one's basic rights from being violated and (2) does not involve illegitimately harming or violating the rights of others. In some circumstances, adequate means of self-defense may require gun ownership and the two qualifications mentioned in the preceding sentence may be met.

Where does this leave us? I will not defend a gun ban both because its consequentialist basis is uncertain and because it is vulnerable to a right-based challenge. I will instead defend gun control. While the consequentialist case for gun control, presented in this chapter, is very strong, gun control opponents may appeal once again to a moral right to gun ownership, claiming that it is not to be overridden on consequentialist grounds. This observation ushers us to the next chapter, where I will consider the gun advocates' appeal to rights as an argument against gun control. There I will engage in argumentative judo, contending that a careful consideration of rights—gun rights, to be sure, but also rights not to be shot and to a safe environment—will ultimately vindicate gun control.

NOTES

1. United Nations Office on Drugs and Crime, "International Rates of Gun Homicides," www.unodc.org, 2011 Excel document accessed January 2, 2014.

2. Erin Richardson and David Hemenway, "Homicide, Suicide, and Unintentional Firearm Fatality: Comparing the United States with Other High-Income Countries, 2003," *Journal of Trauma: Injury, Infection & Critical Care* 70 (2011): 238–43, at 241.

3. For a remarkably comprehensive summary of relevant studies, see Matthew Miller, Deborah Azrael, and David Hemenway, "Firearms and Violent Death in the United States," in Daniel Webster and Jon Vernick, eds., *Gun Violence in America* (Baltimore: Johns Hopkins University Press, 2013), 3–20, at 8–11. For other summary discussions, see David Hemenway, *Private Guns, Public Health* (Ann Arbor: University of Michigan Press, 2010), 45–54; and Philip Cook and Kristin Goss, *The Gun Debate* (New York: Oxford University Press, 2014), 57–59. For some specific studies, see David Lester, "Crime as Opportunity: A Test of the Hypothesis with European Homicide Rates," *British Journal of Criminology* 31 (1991): 186–88; Martin Killias, "International Correlations Between Gun Ownership and Rates of Homicide and Suicide," *Canadian Medical Association Journal* 148 (1993): 1721–25; Centers for Disease Control and Prevention, "Rates of Homicide, Suicide, and Firearm-Related Death Among Children—26 Industrialized Countries," *Morbidity and Mortality Weekly Report* 46 (February 7, 1997): 101–105; David Hemenway and Matthew Miller, "Firearm Availability and Homicide Rates Across 26 High-Income Countries," *Journal of Trauma: Injury, Infection & Critical Care* 49 (2000): 985–88; Matthew Miller, Deborah Azrael, and David Hemenway, "Household Firearm Ownership Levels and Homicide Rates Across U.S. Regions and States, 1988-1997," *American Journal of Public Health* 92 (2002): 1988–93; Martin Killias, "Gun Ownership, Suicide and Homicide: An International Perspective," *Journal of*

ENFORCING RIGHTS NOT TO BE SHOT AND NOT TO BE HARMED THROUGH GROSS NEGLIGENCE

In chapter 11, we found that there was a reasonably strong case for a moral right to gun ownership, at least when that right was properly qualified. The qualifications to the gun right, we found, trace to the qualified right to self-defense on which it rests. The moral right to self-defense includes the freedom to use adequate means to defend oneself— provided that using such means (1) is necessary to prevent one's basic rights from being violated and (2) does not involve illegitimately harming or violating the rights of others. In some circumstances, adequate means of self-defense may require gun ownership and the two conditions mentioned in the preceding sentence may be satisfied. But notice that this basis for a right to own guns *effectively includes a justification for significant gun control in its conditions.* As we found in chapter 11, to meet the conditions just stated requires (1) demonstrating a special need to own a gun, since otherwise defense of one's physical security can be delegated to agents of the government (police and military), and (2) a requirement to pass a gun safety course, so that there is a reasonable expectation that one's possession of a gun will make household members safer rather than less safe. Thus, by qualifying the moral right to self-defense and taking into account relevant empirical data about gun ownership in the United States, we specified the presumed right to own guns in a way that demands significant forms of gun control.

In the present discussion, we can ignore the way in which the strongest case for gun rights, properly interpreted, demands gun control, as just explained. What propels the argument of this chapter is the observation that other moral rights, in addition to the right to bear arms, are relevant to the debate. And we will find that the argument justifies some types of gun control beyond the two just mentioned as connected with the limited scope of the presumed gun right: demonstrated need and completion of a safety course.

One right that is particularly relevant in this context is *the right not to be shot*. For present purposes, let us consider only those potential shooting victims who are not doing something—such as attempting murder, rape, or forcible entry—that might justify their being shot. In other words, we will assume that the potential victims are nonthreatening and have an *undefeated* right (one that is not justifiably overridden) not to be shot. To be sure, the assertion of a right not to be shot may sound odd because it is rarely, if ever, explicitly invoked. But the right is a plausible specification of rights not to be killed or grievously injured—in contexts in which firearms are available. People have a right not to be shot.

Since people have this right, others violate the right if they shoot people. So the right in question entails an obligation on the part of others to refrain from shooting people. But one of the chief legitimating purposes of a state—and therefore the government—is to enforce the law and protect people's rights, so the right not to be shot generates obligations not only on the part of other individuals but also on the part of the government. Thus, if you shoot me (and, again, we assume in this discussion that the shooting victim has done nothing to justify being shot), then the state must make every reasonable effort to apprehend, try, and punish you. This after-the-fact aspect of enforcement of rights is a matter of executing criminal law. But the state also has the job of taking reasonable measures to *prevent* people from shooting others. One's right not to be shot is worthless in practical terms if people can shoot me with little difficulty and impunity. In addition to punishing crimes, the government must try to prevent crime. Of particular relevance to the present discussion is that the police—not to mention other branches of the government[1]—should take reasonable measures to prevent the violation of people's right not to be shot.

Consider the situation of a child living in his parents' house. Obviously, the child has a right not to be shot. If one of his parents goes berserk and shoots him, the child's right is violated. The government should therefore take reasonable measures to make it extremely unlikely that this will happen. Assuming guns are not banned—consistent with the assumption of a right to bear arms—this could take the form of such gun control measures as universal background checks with reasonable criteria for excluding people at high risk of psychological breakdowns. If, alternatively, the child or one of his buddies plays around with the gun and accidentally shoots the child in question, then his right not to be shot has been violated. Even though the shooting in this case is an accident performed by someone too young to bear legal culpability, no one who is incapable of handling guns safely should have had access to firearms in the house. The moral crime here is one of gross negligence leading to the shooting of an innocent victim. Accordingly, it would be appropriate to require safe storage of firearms, gun training, and licensing for anyone who will have access to them, and perhaps safety features that make them unlikely to be fired accidentally. If, to mention a third possibility, the child is shot not by a household member or a friend but by a criminal intruder, the child's right not to be shot has been violated in this case as well. Reasonable prevention of this rights violation would include gun control measures that reduce the possibility of guns getting into criminal hands—universal background checks, again, as well as a prohibition of private gun sales and gifting, measures that make gun trafficking more difficult, and the like. These measures can help to protect people's right not to be shot without violating gun ownership rights.

Here is another way to look at the matter. There are two rights to consider: the right to own guns and the right not to be shot. If there were only the right to own guns and if, as gun proponents often hold, rights trump consequentialist considerations, then the right to own guns would apparently trump such consequentialist considerations as the social costs of widespread gun ownership where there is weak gun control. But there are two rights, so neither right can trump the other. Rather, a responsible delineation of the *scope* of each right must take the other right into due consideration. Because there is a right to own guns, the right not to be shot cannot be protected in ways that obliterate gun rights—say, by banning private gun ownership.[2] Meanwhile, because there is a right not to be shot, the right to own guns cannot be so free of restrictions that the former right becomes, in practical terms, an empty sham—a mere formality like the right to vote of someone who cannot possibly get to a voting station and is not permitted to vote by mail. Appropriate gun control measures limit the scope of the right to own guns in ways that are reasonably responsive to people's right not to be shot. For example, our right not to be shot is unduly and unnecessarily threatened if convicted felons and terrorists may legally purchase guns.[3]

Given that rights cannot trump each other, how should we think about justified ways of delineating the scope of the two rights in question? We may do so in terms of *balancing the interests* associated with each right.[4] Suppose Joe, a father, exercises his right to bear arms and acquires a gun. But Junior, Joe's young son, cannot be trusted to handle a gun safely. Junior, of course, has a right not to be shot. Now suppose Joe loves guns—and hates gun restrictions—so much that he wants to be able to leave his gun lying around the house, even in places where Junior can reach it. Joe has an interest in leaving his gun where he pleases. Junior has an interest (as well as a right) not to be shot. If Joe can leave his gun on the living room coffee table, for example, it would be easy for Junior to get his hands on it—and with only a bit of bad luck, Junior could shoot himself. Junior's interest in not getting shot is far more compelling and substantial than Joe's interest in leaving his gun wherever he pleases. Or, to put the idea in different terms, the *costs* to Junior of Joe's leaving his gun lying around—understood in terms of the risks Junior would face—are much greater than the *costs* to Joe of having to store his gun safely—namely, some inconvenience. Because Joe does not have a *right* to leave his gun wherever he pleases, he cannot claim that his interest in doing so trumps Junior's interest in not being shot or society's interests in the safety of its members. Rather, once again, we must weigh competing interests against each other, and Junior's interest in not being shot is weightier. This legitimates safe storage requirements for guns. Note that such a gun regulation is compatible with Joe's right to own a gun.

In the argument just presented, I suggested a balancing of Joe's and Junior's competing interests, with Junior's interest proving more compelling. If I'm not mistaken, we can advance an even stronger argument. That is because Junior has a right (not just an interest) that would be violated if he were shot. This interest *trumps* Joe's interest in leaving his gun lying around and, more generally, trumps interests (e.g., not to be inconvenienced) that are not protected by rights. If Joe had a *right* to put his gun wherever he pleased, then Junior's right not to be shot would not trump Joe's right. For, in general, rights do not trump each other; rather, where they are in tension, they must take each other into account in delineating their scopes. But Joe has no such right, so Junior's right not to be shot trumps.

One might object to my reference to Junior's right not to be shot in this scenario, in which Joe's lassitude enables Junior to play with the gun and accidentally *shoot himself.* While acknowledging that Junior's right not to be shot would be violated if Joe or an intruder shot Junior, one might doubt that Junior's accidentally shooting himself would entail a violation of his right not to be shot. After all, who violates Junior's right in such a case? It seems odd to claim that Junior violates his own right. But, if not Junior, then who is the rights violator?

The answer, I think, is that Joe violated Junior's moral right and, assuming that no law prohibited Joe's leaving the gun lying around, society also violated Junior's right. Before presenting my argument for this thesis, I acknowledge that it sounds strange to say that Joe and/or society violated Junior's right not to be shot when neither Joe nor society actually shot Junior. For this reason, and without denying the obvious fact that Junior has a right not to be shot, our analysis might best proceed by focusing on a distinct right of Junior's: *the right not to be harmed through gross negligence*. Surely, every child has such a right against his or her parents and society. If this claim does not seem obvious, it should after we consider two further scenarios.

Suppose Ralph has been doing some house cleaning with liquid bleach and leaves it in a bucket on the kitchen floor right next to a set of plastic tea cups belonging to his three-year-old daughter, Rachel. Ralph then goes upstairs to do some computer work, leaving Rachel unattended on the first floor. A half hour later, Rachel finds her way to the kitchen, uses a plastic tea cup to scoop up some bleach, drinks a large mouthful, and becomes violently ill. In another scenario, imagine that Mary purchases and brings home an extremely aggressive pit bull. Despite knowing that the dog is dangerous, especially to small children, she permits her daughter, Molly, to play in the backyard near the pit bull. Molly tries to pat the dog's head only to be mauled, sustaining serious injuries.

In both cases, a child is seriously harmed. The immediate cause of Rachel's poisoning is her drinking liquid bleach. The immediate cause of Molly's injuries is the attack of a pit bull. Yet, in both cases, parents were responsible for protecting their children from known dangers. They failed to take reasonable measures to do so, with the result that their children were seriously harmed. In a morally relevant sense, the parents harmed their children through gross negligence. Perhaps it is also true that the society was seriously negligent in permitting a family with small children to acquire a highly dangerous dog, assuming no law prevented Mary from buying or adopting the pit bull. (In the case of Ralph and Rachel, the society does not seem guilty of negligence unless it had no legal requirements for child-proofing bleach bottles.)

In the case of Junior, analogous judgments make sense. Junior's right not to be harmed through gross negligence was violated by his father and by a society that did not require his father to store his weapon safely. It does not matter whether we also say that Junior's right not to be shot was violated by his father and society. The fact that in this imaginary scenario a rights violation clearly takes place justifies gun control measures that are reasonably related to the task of preventing such tragic rights violations. A prime example of such gun control measures is safe storage requirements.

THE RIGHT TO A SAFE ENVIRONMENT

A somewhat different argumentative path leads to the same conclusion. This argument invokes *a right to a (reasonably) safe environment*. Whereas the right not to be shot is naturally regarded as a negative right—a right not to have something done to one—a right to a safe environment might naturally be construed as a positive right—a right to be provided with some good, in this case a safe environment. (Interestingly, a right not to be harmed through gross negligence seems equally construable as a negative right, if we think of negligence as a kind of wrongful behavior, or as a positive right, if we frame negligence as a failure to perform certain required actions.) The distinction between negative and positive rights is arguably important here insofar as it supports objections to gun control

In calling the American gun policy status quo *extreme*, I use the adjective quite deliberately. To be sure, "extreme" is a term that should be deployed with care, because to call a position or state of affairs extreme in a political or moral context is not only to describe it as very far to one side of a spectrum of viewpoints or possibilities but also to imply that it is "beyond the pale," unreasonable, and indefensible. This is exactly what I mean to say. The American gun policy status quo is thoroughly indefensible. No well-informed, morally serious person could defend it. Maybe such a person could defend certain aspects of the status quo—such as the Supreme Court's assertion of a constitutional right to bear arms—but no well-informed, morally serious person could defend all, or nearly all, of our prevailing gun laws, regulations, and enforcement practices as adequate.

If the American gun status quo is so indefensible, how can one explain it? That is, why *is* it the status quo? How could the United States of America, with a well-respected Constitution and a well-established balance of government powers, produce a major area of public policy that is thoroughly unjustified? In sum, the status quo is explicable by reference to (1) the libertarian streak in American political culture, (2) an increasingly dysfunctional federal government and political system more broadly, and (3) an enormously energetic and powerful gun lobby that has taken an extreme anti-gun control stance in recent decades. Once these factors are understood, the gun policy status quo is not surprising. But, from an ethical standpoint, it remains indefensible.

The purpose of this chapter is to illustrate how one-sided American gun policies are and to elaborate briefly on the aforementioned factors that explain the status quo.

Doing so will allow thoughtful readers to recognize that the current American approach to gun control bears no necessary relation to a morally defensible system of gun control. In this way, the discussion will pave the ground for the final chapter, on policy recommendations. The gun control I recommend is far more extensive than what currently exists in the United States. As this chapter should help to clarify, the distance between what I recommend and the American status quo does not indicate that my proposals are extreme. Rather, this gulf reflects the extreme character of the status quo.

ILLUSTRATIONS OF AN INDEFENSIBLE STATUS QUO

Rather than providing a comprehensive overview of the American gun status quo, I will present illustrations that help to characterize it as extremely friendly to gun owners, gun sellers, gun manufacturers, and politicians who support these constituents and extremely unfriendly to gun control, the politicians who would like to support it, and gun-related law enforcement. Each illustration is stated as a blunt fact (in an italicized sentence) and some are followed by a brief comment.

1. *Due to the "gun show loophole"—the exemption of guns sold privately from the federal requirement of background checks on prospective buyers—sellers may legally sell firearms to the following groups of individuals so long as they do not share the information that would exclude them: terrorists, individuals convicted*

of illogic apparently encouraged by the gun lobby. That the dealers planned to sell smart guns along with, and not in place of, traditional firearms was not enough to placate the intimidating gun enthusiasts.

14. *The sensibilities of (many) American gun enthusiasts are so extreme that a pre-eminent gun journalist, who had long written a column for* Gun & Ammo *magazine, was ostracized for suggesting in a column that gun rights needed to be limited.* As a reporter put it: "The backlash was swift and fierce. Readers threatened to cancel their subscriptions. Death threats poured in by email. His television program was pulled from the air."[16] Yet his statement about regulations was essentially the same as the very Supreme Court decision that affirmed a constitutional right to bear arms: Gun rights and gun control are compatible.

15. *Colorado Senate President John Morse and State Senator Angela Giron were forced out of office by successful recalls simply because they supported Colorado's new gun laws, which required background checks for all gun purchases, limited the size of ammunition magazines, and the like.* These punishments reflect the extraordinary political power of the gun lobby, which got its membership to the polls to vote for the recall. Colorado is home to two of the worst gun massacres in recent American history, the second of which (recounted in chapter 9) helped to spur the new legislation.[17]

These facts about the U.S. gun status quo are remarkable. They reflect a pro-gun extremism in American gun policy and gun culture. It is worth considering, however briefly, leading factors that contribute to this state of affairs.

EXPLAINING AMERICAN EXTREMISM ABOUT GUNS

As mentioned earlier, three important factors contribute to the pro-gun extremism found in the United States: the pronounced libertarian streak in American political culture, a dysfunctional federal government, and an extraordinarily effective gun lobby.

Libertarianism is the political and moral philosophy that prioritizes liberty over other values, including individual welfare and societal utility, and asserts the existence of various negative rights—or rights of noninterference—while denying the existence of such putative positive rights as rights to subsistence, shelter, and health care.[18] For the libertarian, human beings have rights to life, liberty, and property. As rights of noninterference, these are rights not to be deprived of one's life, liberty, or property, not rights to have one's live saved through the provision of health care, to have one's options expanded through social supports, or to be provided with property. Libertarianism, thus understood, fits nicely with the image of rugged Americans settling new frontiers and taking care of themselves without help from the government or charities. Despite the fact that the United States currently has a partial welfare state—with entitlements to public schooling, food assistance,

Medicare, and Social Security, among other goods—the image of the tough, self-reliant American endures in the popular imagination, especially among Americans who are relatively conservative and suspicious of government intrusion in citizens' lives.

As discussed in chapter 14, libertarianism—at least in a relatively pure form—is deeply implausible. But few Americans are true (pure) libertarians. Instead, many Americans are libertarian-*leaning*. This rightward inclination appears much more common in the United States than in other developed countries, an observation that helps to explain why our gun policy status quo is so extreme. Americans are more likely to enact, and tolerate, policies that prioritize liberty rights—in this case, the right to private gun ownership—over concerns about public safety and, more generally, the common good. Liberty rights take priority over societal utility.

But to emphasize the libertarian streak in American political culture is to risk a distortion: the impression that Americans actually accept the gun policy status quo. Americans strongly tend to believe in gun rights, but they also believe in gun control far more than is reflected in current gun policies. The vast majority of Americans, for example, support universal background checks, yet federal law persists in featuring an exemption of private sales from the requirement to conduct such checks. In this way, even the libertarian-leaning American public is in the position of being dissatisfied with the paucity of commonsense gun regulations, as illustrated in the preceding section. How to account for this disconnect between what the American public believes and wants regarding gun control and the meager gun regulations on the books? This is where the other two aforementioned factors prove especially relevant.

One of these factors is the increasingly dysfunctional American federal government. Currently, Congress is rarely able to pass legislation in the public interest if the legislation is opposed by powerful special-interest groups. Several problems are especially noteworthy. First, it is enormously expensive to run for political office, so viable candidates need a great deal of funding, which wealthy special-interest groups are better able to provide than poor special-interest groups. As a result, Big Pharma, the private health insurance industry, the agricultural lobby, bankers, the American Israel Public Affairs Committee (AIPAC), and, of course, the gun lobby have outsized influence on American legislators and presidents. Much of the outsized influence is due to the U.S. Supreme Court's decision in *Citizens United*, which undid the campaign finance reform that was aimed at curbing the influence of wealthy special interests. In any case, wealthy special-interest groups can block legislation that runs counter to their financial or political interests by coopting politicians who depend on generous contributions in order to be (re)elected. In the House of Representatives, the situation is worsened by redistricting within states, which has the effect of favoring more ideologically committed (as opposed to pragmatic and centrist) candidates. These individuals are more likely to oppose legislation that runs counter to their ideology than individuals, formerly better represented in the House, who are open to compromise. Meanwhile, the Senate is even less capable of passing important legislation that enjoys broad public support because filibusters—which can be ended only by 60 votes from the 100-member chamber— can prevent bills from being discussed and voted on. All these factors contribute to a highly dysfunctional federal government, which in turn helps explain our extreme, indefensible gun policy status quo.

The dysfunctional political system, as just mentioned, features political lobbies with outsized influence. One of these, the gun lobby, deserves a moment in the sunshine of this discussion. Although the NRA is sometimes taken to be *the* gun lobby, pro-gun American organizations also include the Gun Owners of America, the National Association for Gun Rights, the Citizens Committee for the Right to Keep and Bear Arms, and others. The NRA, however, is by far the most powerful of these organizations, enjoying a prominent place at the table when major firearms legislation is being considered. So powerful is the NRA's influence in the halls of Congress that one Democratic staffer, speaking on the condition of anonymity, stated, "We do absolutely anything they ask and WE NEVER cross them. . . . Pandering to the NRA is probably the worst part of my job."[19]

Why is the NRA so powerful? Several factors merit mention. First, the organization was able to grow its membership in no small measure because, in the late nineteenth century and for much of the twentieth century, it received substantial subsidies from the federal government (for example, to promote marksmanship)[20]—an ironic fact, considering the organization's usual anti-government tone in communicating with its membership. Second, the NRA has a simple, unifying message that all members— estimates vary, but the number is somewhere between 3 and 5 million—can understand: "Any new gun regulations would threaten your gun rights; compromising in any way that permits more gun control strengthens those who favor banning firearms in the U.S." The NRA's Institute for Legislative Action (ILA), created in 1975—around the time the NRA transformed from a moderate organization that promoted hunters' interests and supported gun control to an organization opposed to virtually all limits to gun rights[21]—is proficient at reaching members with legislative alerts of the form, "Get to the polls and vote against [so-and-so], who wants to take away your guns."[22] Third, gun advocates are apparently more likely to take action—writing a letter, giving money, or even voting for a candidate exclusively on the basis of her position on gun control—than are gun opponents.[23] Fourth, the organization is effective in applying direct pressure on lawmakers at the federal, state, and local levels. Fifth, because the NRA's unifying message is negative—opposition to gun control—it has a built-in political advantage over efforts to expand gun control: in the American political system, as discussed earlier, it's much easier to block legislation than to enact it.

In view of these three main factors—a libertarian-leaning political culture, a dysfunctional political system that is biased against the passing of new laws, and an enormously powerful gun lobby—the U.S. gun policy status quo is not so surprising. Yet it remains indefensible. The status quo serves the interests of the gun lobby, gun makers and sellers, and the politicians who protect their interests at the expense of the public at large. In the final chapter, I propose specific departures from the status quo.

NOTES

1. Philip Cook and Jens Ludwig, *Guns in America* (Washington, DC: Police Foundation, 1996).

that one's job—say, in security or espionage—presents a special need for a handgun.

2. *Those who demonstrate special need for a gun should have to pass a rigorous training course on firearm use and safety before obtaining a license.* We require extensive training for individuals to obtain drivers' licenses. We should do the same for gun licenses. Providing some international perspective, Australia, Belgium, Canada, France, Japan, New Zealand, Norway, and Spain all require successful completion of gun training as a condition for obtaining a gun license.[5]

3. *No one should be legally permitted to purchase, own, or use a gun prior to age 21.* Here we should parallel the age-based legal restriction on purchase and use of alcohol, a restriction that saves lives. (One possible exception regarding *use* of guns is that minors may be permitted to use guns for target practice on approved, well-supervised shooting ranges.)

4. *Laws should stipulate that only properly licensed adults may use a gun, and that one may not use someone else's gun except in a life-threatening emergency calling for forceful defense.* (The possible exception noted in 3 applies here as well.)

5. *Guns should be acquirable only from federally licensed dealers while private sales and the gifting of guns should be illegal.*

6. *Federally licensed dealers should be permitted to sell a firearm to a given individual only after completing a criminal and psychiatric background check (no exceptions).*

7. *The categories of ineligibility to purchase a firearm should be expanded from the current narrow criteria— roughly, a felony conviction, hospitalization for psychiatric illness, dishonorable discharge from the military, or being a fugitive from justice—to include the following categories:*

   a. *Gang membership (as determined by a judge)*

   b. *Conviction for drug or gun trafficking*

   c. *Conviction for more than one crime involving alcohol or illegal drugs within a three-year period (ineligible for ten years)*

   d. *Documented dangerousness to self or others (although reporting laws must be carefully crafted to protect psychiatric patients' confidentiality) or having been found, in a court of law, not guilty by reason of insanity*

   e. *Being under a temporary restraining order filed for threat of violence*

   f. *Conviction of a violent misdemeanor (fifteen years of ineligibility), any violent crime as a minor (ineligible until age 30), misdemeanor stalking, or violation of a restraining order issued due to a threat of violence.*[6]

Law Enforcement

8. *Appointment of an ATF Director should not require U.S. Senate confirmation.* Senate confirmation was a procedural anomaly created as part of a wish list of the National Rifle Association, which wanted power to block any nominated director from

assuming the position. It has no justification and potentially cripples law enforcement.

9. *ATF must be properly funded so it can do its job effectively.*

10. *Two impediments to law enforcement imposed by the Firearm Owners' Protection Act—limiting the ATF to one inspection of gun dealers per year and increased evidentiary standards (e.g., proving unlawful intent) for prosecuting dealers who conduct illegal sales—should be rescinded.*[7]

11. *The Protection of Lawful Commerce in Arms Act, which arbitrarily freed gun dealers and manufacturers from any tort liability, should be repealed.*[8]

12. *All federal restrictions on access to firearm tracing data, except for those connected with ongoing criminal investigations, should be repealed.*[9]

13. *All guns made or sold after a specified date should be required to have effective tracing mechanisms.*

14. *A national database of gun sales and gun owners should be established and effectively maintained.* Like the other measures listed in this section, the purposes are accountability and effective law enforcement.

Research

15. *The federal government should permit and adequately fund the Centers for Disease Control and Prevention, the National Institutes of Health, and the National Institute of Justice to conduct high-quality research on the causes of gun violence, the promise and limits*

of various regulations for reducing gun violence, and similar matters.[10]

16. *The surgeon general should regularly report on the state of the problem of American gun violence and any progress that has been made in addressing the problem.*[11]

Banning of Excessively Dangerous Weaponry

17. *The federal government should ban future sale of assault weapons, with a better definition—not riddled with loopholes—than the one included in the 1994 Assault Weapons Ban. Those who already own these weapons legally will not be required to relinquish them.*

18. *Future sale of high-capacity magazine clips, defined as those carrying more than ten rounds of ammunition, should be banned.*

19. *Future sale of any kind of armor-piercing ("cop-killer") bullets should be banned.*

20. *Payment should be offered for voluntary forfeiture of assault weapons, high-capacity clips, or armor-piercing bullets that had been legally purchased before the bans became effective. Because such a buyback program would be voluntary, it would reward responsible behavior without limiting anyone's options.*

Removal and Prohibition of Physician "Gag Orders"

21. *Laws that prevent physicians from discussing the risks of firearm ownership and the importance of firearm safety with their patients should be prohibited.*

Safety of Guns in Homes and as Consumer Products

22. *Federal legislation requiring safe storage of firearms in the home should be enacted.*

23. *The Federal Consumer Product Commission should receive authority to regulate firearms and ammunition as consumer products.*

24. *Congress should provide grants to spur further development of personalized (smart) guns, which can only be fired by their owners.*[12]

25. *Congress should provide states financial incentives to require childproof or personalized guns.*[13]

I submit these recommendations in full awareness that most or all of them are now politically infeasible. This is a book about ethics and, in particular, morally justified gun policy. In such a discussion, it is paramount to distinguish what is ethically sound from what is politically feasible. If the arguments in this part of the book have been largely sound, then the recommendations of this chapter represent, at least roughly, the direction in which the United States should move. Presently, as discussed in the previous chapter, we have a dysfunctional federal government that has trouble passing sensible legislation, a political system biased in the favor of wealthy special interests, and a cynical gun lobby that has intimidated politicians into passing and maintaining extreme gun laws that disserve the American public. It is uncertain when we will see a better day. But every morally serious American should call for the enactment of sensible gun policies. Consistent with the idea animating the development of this book, clear thinking about the issue is a first step.

NOTES

1. A reviewer of a draft of this volume complained that I had cited no empirical studies demonstrating the cost-effectiveness of the measures I propose. But I reject the idea that Americans should wait around for the completion of studies of cost-effectiveness before enacting commonsense gun regulations and making our gun policy approach less extreme. I am fairly sure—and glad—that Americans did not await cost-effectiveness studies before requiring drivers to obtain driving permits and cars to include seatbelts. Nevertheless, for discussions of evidence that tend to support my confidence in the cost-effectiveness of gun control, see Philip Cook and Kristin Goss, *The Gun Debate* (New York: Oxford University Press, 2014), ch. 7; and Daniel Webster and Jon Vernick, eds., *Reducing Gun Violence in America: Informing Policy with Evidence and Analysis* (Baltimore: Johns Hopkins University Press, 2013).

2. See Steven Weinberger, David Hoyt, Hal Lawrence, et al., "Firearm-Related Injury and Death in the United States: A Call to Action from 8 Health Professional Organizations and the American Bar Association," *Annals of Internal Medicine* 162 (2015): 513–16, at 514.

3. Jon Vernick, James Hodge, and Daniel Webster, "The Ethics of Restrictive Licensing for Handguns: Comparing the United States and Canadian Approaches to Handgun Regulation," *Journal of Law, Medicine & Ethics* 35 (Winter 2007): 668–78, at 670.

4. David Hemenway, *Private Guns, Public Health* (Ann Arbor: University of Michigan Press, 2004), 198.

5. Ibid.

6. I am heavily indebted to a list of expanded categories presented in "Consensus Recommendations for Reforms to Federal Gun Policies," in Webster and Vernick, *Reducing Gun Violence in America*, 260–61.

7. Ibid, 161.

8. Ibid.

9. Ibid.